Perspectives
on Identity Theft

Crime Prevention Studies
Volume 23

Ronald V. Clarke, series editor

Perspectives on Identity Theft

edited by
Megan M. McNally
and Graeme R. Newman

LYNNE
RIENNER
PUBLISHERS

BOULDER
LONDON

Published in the United States of America in 2010 by
Lynne Rienner Publishers, Inc.
1800 30th Street, Boulder, Colorado 80301
www.rienner.com

and in the United Kingdom by
Lynne Rienner Publishers, Inc.
3 Henrietta Street, Covent Garden, London WC2E 8LU

ISBN: 978-1-881798-80-4 (hc : alk. paper)
ISBN: 978-1-881798-81-1 (pb : alk. paper)
LC: 2008298331

First published in 2008 by Criminal Justice Press.
Reprinted here from the original edition.

Printed and bound in the United States of America

 The paper used in this publication meets the requirements
of the American National Standard for Permanence of
Paper for Printed Library Materials Z39.48-1992.

5 4 3 2 1

CONTENTS

continued

Contents

EDITORS' INTRODUCTION

by

Megan M. McNally
School of Criminal Justice
Rutgers University, Newark

Graeme R. Newman
School of Criminal Justice
University at Albany

Identity theft has existed for centuries, but the opportunities for its commission have evolved over time as a function of modernization. While concern for the problem has mounted steadily since the dawn of the information age, it first began to crystallize during the 1990s. Despite the sheer amount of attention this issue has received over the past decade, especially with regard to the steps that individuals should take to prevent their own victimization, there has been a glaring lack of scholarly attention as a whole – an omission that this volume of *Crime Prevention Studies* attempts to redress. In order to contextualize what each contributing author adds to this field, however, it is first necessary to provide a brief background on the issue of identity theft.[1]

The Definition of Identity Theft

Although there has never been a consensus with regard to what identity theft is, this concept generally refers to an instance in which an individual's personal information is used by another to facilitate an act of fraud. The terms *identity theft* and *identity fraud* are often used interchangeably, as

Crime Prevention Studies, volume 23 (2008), pp. 1–8.

they are in the chapters in this volume, but they have also been viewed as separate yet related offense categories. The primary reasons for this are twofold. Historically, *identity fraud* was viewed as being committed against the collective bodies (e.g., governments, financial institutions) that received fraudulent personal information rather than against the people who were fraudulently identified by that information. The term *identity theft*, which did not appear until the late 1980s,[2] was initially used to distinguish individual victims (identity theft) from collective victims (identity fraud) – both of whom were harmed by the same set of criminal activities. More recently, these terms have been applied in a different manner to separate the act of acquiring an individual's personal information (identity theft) from the act of misusing that information (identity fraud); however, since obtaining someone's personal information (e.g., social security number, credit card account number) is a necessary condition for its misuse, many tend to call this combined act *identity theft*. The chapters in this volume therefore deal with both the acquisition (theft) and illicit use (fraud) of identity information.

The misuse of an individual's personal information can also occur in one of two basic ways. Offenders can either access an individual's existing accounts or use another's personal information to open new accounts and/ or aid in the commission of other types of fraud. The bulk of identity theft consists of instances in which a victim's personal accounts (i.e., resulting from contracts that s/he has willingly and knowingly entered into, such as credit card accounts, checking or savings accounts, and insurance policies) are compromised by an offending party who has access to pertinent information. The most threatening form of identity theft, sometimes known as "true-name" fraud, occurs when an offender literally assumes another individual's identity to lead a life parallel to the victim's. For example, such offenders can initiate contracts for new accounts of various types, and/or apply for employment, housing and government benefits or provide authorities with their "new" name to escape punishment and avoid detection. Since victims may remain unaware of these activities for extended periods of time, there are often severe consequences associated with this form of identity theft victimization. Although it has sometimes been argued that the term *identity theft* should be reserved for the activities involved in true-name fraud, while the term *identity fraud* should be used for offenses that affect a victim's existing personal accounts, the contributions in this volume are intended to enhance the understanding of identity theft in all of its forms.

The Extent of Identity Theft

It is frequently acknowledged that the present-day specter of identity theft comprises various acts that have long been criminal in the eyes of American law. First recognized as a separate offense by Arizona in 1996, however, identity theft had been criminalized in some form by 2005 within every U.S. state and the District of Columbia, and under federal law. As directed by the Identity Theft and Assumption Deterrence Act of 1998 (Public Law 105-318), the Federal Trade Commission (FTC) began to collect complaint data and provide identity theft information to the public in 1999 through its newly created Identity Theft Clearinghouse (ITC). The ITC, which is currently the only centralized repository for identity theft complaints in the U.S., has since collected over 1 million reports, ranging from a low of 31,117 in 2000 to a high of 255,613 in 2005. These figures steadily increased between 2000 and 2005, but the last published figure for 2006 (246,035) may represent either the beginning of a decline or a leveling off in reporting given its similarity to the figure reported for 2004 (246,882).[3]

The first nationally representative study of this phenomenon, conducted in 2003 on behalf of the FTC (Synovate, 2003), concluded that slightly more than 27 million U.S. adults had been victimized by some form of identity theft during the five-year period between March/April 1998 and March/April 2003. This survey has since been replicated annually by an independent research firm – Javelin Strategy & Research – which has consistently reported a decrease in identity theft victimization over the past few years: 10.1 million U.S. adults in 2003, 9.3 million in 2004, 8.9 million in 2005, 8.4 million in 2006, and 8.1 million in 2007 (Javelin Strategy & Research, 2008).[4]

The National Crime Victimization Survey (NCVS), like the FTC and Javelin studies, also obtains data from a representative sample of U.S. residents. Identity theft questions were recently added to the NCVS, but the results so far have been published separately from its overall findings on national crime victimization; as a result, the relationship between identity theft and the other forms of crime measured by the NCVS is unclear. According to its findings, however, 3.1% of all U.S. households (3.5 million) were victimized by identity theft during a 6-month period in 2004 (Baum, 2006) and 5.5% of all U.S. households (6.4 million) were victimized by identity theft between January and December 2005 (Baum, 2007). It is, nevertheless, difficult to compare these estimates with the findings from the FTC and Javelin victimization surveys, first because of the difference in measurement units (i.e., households in the NCVS as opposed to individuals in the other two surveys), and second because the 2004 estimate from the NCVS is based on six months' worth of data, rather than one full year.

Results from all three of these victim surveys must be treated with some caution since each measures identity theft victimizations that both are, and are not, reported to the police. In comparison with other types of offending, identity theft victimization reporting patterns are complicated by the fact that these victims often need to contact a non-law enforcement agency for help (e.g., a credit bureau, or the company that issued an account); thus, many victims are able to resolve the issue without having to involve the police. As a result, victimization surveys such as those performed by Javelin and the NCVS represent the uppermost limit of identity theft victimization in the U.S., while the Uniform Crime Reports will reveal the lowest total once police reporting procedures have been standardized. Much of what we currently know about identity theft, however, currently comes from information provided by the victims of this offense – whether this be through a victimization survey or as a result of their request for assistance to various agencies such as the FTC's Identity Theft Clearinghouse.

The Commission of Identity Theft

Although valuable, victim reports are often incomplete with regard to the processes or methods involved in their victimization. Approximately half of all victims, for example, report being aware of how their personal information was obtained. While the majority of these victims report that the information used to commit identity theft was obtained through some type of non-technology-based method (e.g., through a lost/stolen wallet or mail, or by culling through their garbage), the large number of victims who are unaware of how their information was initially obtained leaves much room for speculation about whether technology-based methods were employed (e.g., computers, the Internet). A minority of victims (approximately 25%) also reports knowing who misused their information, but certain categories of offenders (e.g., friends, family members, acquaintances) may be disproportionately over-reported by victims due to the physical and psychological proximity inherent to these types of relationships. The large percentage of offenders who are unknown to their victims has sometimes been interpreted to show that anonymous technology-based methods were used to commit these offenses, but there is not enough evidence to support or refute this view at the present time.

While definitive answers regarding the role of technology in either the acquisition or misuse of personal information are not currently available, it is clear that the contemporary problem of identity theft has been fueled by changes in the ways that personal information is used, stored and transmitted within modern societies. Other factors, such as an increasing reliance on credit and the usurpation of the social security number in America as a primary means for identification, have also converged to help form the foundation upon which identity theft can be accomplished. Although the contributions in this volume only touch upon the complex underpinnings of this collective problem, each is an essential first step toward understanding identity theft more completely and responding more effectively in order to prevent its occurrence.

THE CONTENTS OF THIS VOLUME

This volume of *Crime Prevention Studies* houses a mix of chapters that explore current theory, research and practice regarding the issue of identity theft. The first two chapters are theoretical in scope. Graeme Newman begins with an overview of the opportunity perspective and its application to the study of identity theft. His discussion explores the allure and ease of this offense, with a particular focus on the role of technology in the creation of opportunities for the acquisition and misuse of personal information. This chapter also lays out the foundations of situational crime prevention (SCP) – a common thread running through several of the contributions. Next, Megan McNally examines the meaning and mechanics of identity theft through use of the "script" approach (Cornish, 1994). Her analysis focuses on deconstructing this phenomenon in order to draft a conceptual map of the topic and to identify the opportunities available for research and prevention. Both of these chapters also provide more detailed background information, which serves to flesh out some of the issues mentioned above in this introduction.

The next two contributions present the results of different types of research projects. The chapter by Henry Pontell, Gregory Brown and Anastasia Tosouni outlines new findings from victimization data collected by the Identity Theft Resource Center – an independent non-profit agency devoted to helping victims of this offense and providing information to the public. This contribution is an important example of creating new opportunities for research in order to guide prevention. Their discussion further highlights the ongoing imbalance within popular discourse between the need for individuals to protect themselves against identity theft and the need for industry members to prevent its occurrence on their behalf. The chapter by Pontell et al. also shows how victimization data can be used to structure future interventions. Next, in one of the few studies of its kind, the chapter by Heith Copes and Lynne Vieraitis explores the commission of identity theft from the offender's perspective. Their findings on the motivations, strategies and skills of identity thieves are used to suggest areas where SCP techniques might be successful in reducing the incidence of identity theft.

Bridging the gap between research and practice is Michael Levi's account of the evolution of identity fraud in the United Kingdom and the programs that have been designed to combat it. This chapter illustrates the international aspects of identity theft, and underscores the similarities and differences between the experiences of the U.K. and the U.S. Levi's analysis further describes the struggle to effect change in the area of plastic card fraud, and emphasizes the universality of some fraud prevention methods. In the next chapter, Russell Smith presents a framework for evaluating preventative interventions related to the challenges of identification. Particular attention is given to the costs and benefits of document-based systems, biometric technologies and identity cards. His discussion also underlines the need to exercise rational choice in the selection of prevention measures, guided by sound research and a consideration of their potential consequences.

The final two chapters focus on understanding how the 25 techniques of situational crime prevention (Cornish and Clarke, 2003) can be used to address the problems underlying identity theft. Sara Berg explores how information technology (IT) can be used in the fight against identity theft. The utility of this approach is demonstrated through the application of eight SCP techniques, using a range of examples from individual to industry prevention. Her discussion also considers the Achilles' heel of technology – human error – and what this might ultimately mean for the effectiveness and future of IT. Finally, Robert Willison examines the use of SCP in the context of information systems security, with a particular emphasis on the "insider" threat posed by employee computer crime. In particular, Willison integrates SCP techniques with the use of "offense scripts" (Cornish, 1994) in order to show how these approaches can work together to strengthen the practices associated with information security, and thereby protect the sensitive personal information that can be used for committing identity theft.

Although the contributions in this volume originate from somewhat different perspectives, all supply something new to our knowledge of identity theft. Several common issues (in addition to SCP) are also addressed throughout the chapters, including definitions, measurement, the scarcity of data, the role of technology, and the importance of cooperation, just to name a few. When read individually, each chapter offers a glimpse into the world of identity theft. When read as a whole, however, this volume captures the diverse dimensions of this topic and the commitment of its contributing authors to understanding identity theft and preventing its occurrence. It is hoped that these pages will inspire others to ask additional questions about what identity theft is and how we should respond to it.

Address correspondence to: MeganM.McNally@gmail.com

NOTES

1. The overview in this chapter is largely based upon the research conducted by Newman and McNally (2005) and McNally (2008), which focused on the development of this issue in the U.S. While three of the chapters in this volume were written by our international compatriots, it is not possible to provide a global history within this introduction; indeed, nothing of this nature currently exists. Many of the issues discussed nevertheless apply in varying degrees to the experiences of other countries.

2. The first-known published use of this term is from a Florida newspaper (Billington, 1989), although earlier records may exist. See McNally (2008) for further information on the history of identity theft and related terminology.

3. These figures were obtained from the annual reports published by the Federal Trade Commission (2007, 2003). The Identity Theft Clearinghouse continually receives data and updates its statistics from previous years within each new annual report, so these numbers are the most recent available.

4. Javelin specifically uses the term *identity fraud* to describe its research, even though it continues the *identity theft* research started by the FTC.

The FTC also recently commissioned a second study (Synovate, 2007), which concluded that 8.3 million U.S. adults had been victimized by some form of identity theft in 2005. The disparity between the figures reported by Javelin (8.9 million) and the FTC (8.3 million) for this year is likely the result of methodological differences. Another figure commonly reported from the original FTC study (Synovate, 2003) is that 9.91 million U.S. adults were victimized during a one-year period ending in March/April 2003. Javelin later reported that 10.1 million U.S. adults had been victimized during 2003, which is attributable to their collection of additional data through the end of that year.

REFERENCES

Baum, K. (2006). *Identity theft, 2004.* Washington, DC: U.S. Bureau of Justice Statistics.

Baum, K. (2007). *Identity theft, 2005.* Washington, DC: U.S. Bureau of Justice Statistics.

Billington, M. (1989, July 6). "Identity theft besmirches victims' records." *Sun-Sentinel,* p. 1B.

Cornish, D. (1994). The procedural analysis of offending and its relevance for situational prevention. In R.V. Clarke (ed.), *Crime Prevention Studies,* vol. 3, pp. 151-196. Monsey, NY: Criminal Justice Press.

Cornish, D. and R. Clarke (2003). "Opportunities, precipitators and criminal decisions: A reply to Wortley's critique of situational crime prevention." In M. Smith and D. Cornish (eds.), *Theory for Practice in Situational Crime Prevention.* (Crime Prevention Studies, vol. 16, pp. 41-96.) Monsey, NY: Criminal Justice Press.

Federal Trade Commission (2003). *National and state trends in fraud & identity theft, January – December 2002.* Washington, DC.

Federal Trade Commission (2007). *Consumer fraud and identity theft complaint data, January – December 2006.* Washington, DC.

Javelin Strategy & Research (2008). *2008 identity fraud survey report: Identity fraud continues to decline, but criminals more effective at using all channels.* Pleasanton, CA.

McNally, M. M. (2008). *Trial by circumstance: Is identity theft a modern-day moral panic?* Unpublished Ph.D. dissertation, Rutgers University.

Newman, G.R. and M.M. McNally (2005). *Identity theft literature review.* Unpublished report prepared for the U.S. National Institute of Justice.

Synovate (2003). *Federal Trade Commission – Identity theft survey report.* McLean, VA.

Synovate (2007). *Federal Trade Commission – 2006 identity theft survey report.* McLean, VA.

IDENTITY THEFT AND OPPORTUNITY

by

Graeme R. Newman
School of Criminal Justice
University at Albany

Abstract: *This chapter explores opportunities for the commission and prevention of identity theft, with a particular focus on the role of technology in both. Identity information is a hot product in contemporary societies, and there are many opportunities to obtain it and misuse it. There are potentially just as many opportunities to prevent either of these activities, however. The allure of this offense is therefore examined through the CRAVED and SCAREM models, and initial consideration is given to the reduction of criminal opportunities for identity theft through the techniques of situational crime prevention. While preventive efforts ultimately need to be tailored for different types of opportunities, the current discussion outlines what this will entail.*

INTRODUCTION: PERSONAL INFORMATION AS THE TARGET OF THEFT

Ever since the recording of births and deaths began, and ever since individuals and groups started living continuously (more or less) in specific locations that came – with the invention of the postal services – to be identified by names and numbers, individuals have acquired identities rooted in these fundamental cornerstones of modern society. The opportunity to steal these identities, therefore, has always been there. The onset of today's information society has pushed all kinds of information to the fore, has transported information from the dusty file cabinets of bureaucracies (both governmental and private) into a major product of the marketplace, so that it has taken on the characteristics of other products of the marketplace that have traditionally been the targets of thieves. Thus, the British Crime Survey (Home Office, 2004) has shown a clear decline in burglary in recent years, a decline which is reasonably attributed to two factors: (1) small household items like electronic goods, such as VCRs, now are too cheap to steal, and (2) those that are valuable, such as high-tech TVs, are too big to steal. Instead, credit cards and wallets have become more popular targets of burglars, even more than jewelry, their traditionally favored target ("The decline of the English burglary," 2004).

Many argue that identity theft is really composed of assorted old crimes using new tools. Fraud, theft, forgery, counterfeiting, traditional cons and scams, fraudulent marketing and many more offenses may all contribute to identity theft, and all are easily adapted to the inviting environment of the information age, as will be noted below. But why should identities, of all things, be targeted, rather than, say, an expensive flat panel TV in a person's home? The short answer is that the latter item may well be targeted, but the way to reach this target is through an individual's identity. The reason for this is simple. Amazon.com's merchandise is hidden away in colossal warehouses (theirs and their clients'), which are not open to the public as in a retail store. And in retail stores, expensive TV sets are very hard to carry away. Why not steal someone's identity and have the TV set delivered to one's door? For this, and other reasons to be recounted below, identities are prime targets of thieves.

But a thief must have some idea of what it is that he is stealing. Is an identity just like any other product that is available to steal: a car, a TV set? In fact, identities are not that different from cars in their availability to steal, except that there are many more of them. Furthermore there are formal ways in which people are attached to their identities as they are attached to their cars. There are procedures that register a car in the name of the owner, and bureaucracies that issue owners' certificates. There are formal procedures that attach a biological individual to a certificate that says who he or she is, a birth certificate when born for example, and later, a photograph on a passport. It is not too big a leap therefore, to think of identities as products that are attractive to thieves just like cars; indeed, even parts of identities such as credit card numbers or passwords are commonly stolen just like car parts.

Newman and Clarke (2003), in their analysis of e-commerce crime, argued that the "hot product" of the information age is information itself, and that the tool offenders increasingly use to access this target is the Internet environment. The hot product of information is composed of many attractive bits of information: bank account numbers, social security numbers, credit card numbers, dates of birth and so on. It remains for the creativity of the thief to turn these bits of information into cash, or something to be used to advantage. Since a person's identity is composed primarily of information, it is but a small step to analyze identity as a "hot product." Identities, however, are complex pieces of information, more so than cars.[1]

What exactly is stolen in an identity theft? There are many different ways to answer this question, depending on the perspective. The popular view of identity is that it is primarily a term used by individuals to refer to themselves as "a person" and used by others to identify them as unique or particular individuals. It is the idea that identity is a psychological construct that lies at the base of the claim that individual victims of identity theft have lost something more than simply money or suffered much more than the annoyance of having to straighten out their credit records and bank accounts: something bad has happened to their good names.[2] However, it is also obvious that the idea of an identity as purely psychological, and perhaps philosophical or even spiritual, is hard to conceptualize as an object of theft. This is because it is intangible and can only be known, ultimately, by the person, the "self."[3]

Everyday life, however, simplifies these philosophical concerns by assigning names to individuals to which they learn to answer. A person's identity as far as everyday life is concerned therefore starts at birth, or very soon after, when the parents give a name to the child, which is in most societies backed up by the authority of the state (or other body with authority, such as a church) with a certificate establishing an individual's identity. This is the universal bedrock of identity, which may explain why the "date of birth" is considered a prime piece of information when issuing various types of individual accounts. And this is why just this one piece of information is truly hot for theft, because it can open the doors to many other pieces of personal information that are almost always authenticated by this basic piece of personal history. Of course, a date of birth is not enough to establish identity. It must be linked directly to the event that made it possible: the birth itself.

Opportunities for Theft in the Authentication Process

Thus, the authentication of an identity requires two primary parts of an identity: biology (what we are, revealed at the biological moment of birth) and life history (who we are). In order to authenticate an identity we must be able to assess each of the two, and then clearly establish the link between them. This is a difficult task. We know, for example, that individuals have many attributes that are unique to them, such as retinal patterns, fingerprints, and DNA. Verifying the name of this unique person is the problem. Our meager attempt in the marketplace to link what we are to who we are is typically a photograph of the individual attached to a piece of paper or plastic, issued by an authoritative body that depends on documents issued by other authoritative bodies that issue documents pertaining to the applicant's life history. There are basically four sources of these: public databases (records of birth, marriage, tax records etc.), commercial databases (energy or telephone bills, mortgage papers), professional and employment history (school or university, educational degrees), and family records (family referees, parents or guardians). A short list of documents deriving from these sources includes (Jones and Levi, 2000):

- Social security card
- Electoral register entries
- Mortgage account information
- Property ownership and lease-hold
- Credit card account and other financial facilities information
- Insurance policies
- Marriage and financial associations
- Higher educational qualifications
- Payment systems facilities – debit/credit/check/charge cards, virtual wallets, "PayPal," etc.
- Energy and tax bills
- Passport
- Employment information from applications for financial services
- Previous addresses
- Previous authentication events
- Telephone numbers – fixed and mobile
- Library cards and other memberships
- Records of birth, marriage and death
- E-mail address
- Forwarding addresses – re-directions
- Health insurance cards
- Driving license

One can see, however, that there is a circularity in this authentication process. Which documents provide more authenticity than others? Which are "primary" and which are "secondary"? Very few, if any, are truly primary; that is, providing a direct link between who one is and what one is. Thus, the great difficulty in establishing a primary document that links the life history of the individual to his or her biology is a very serious point of weakness in establishing identity. If an offender can obtain just one or two of these documents, it is possible to "breed" additional documents.

The short list of sources above also shows clearly that very large amounts of personal information reside in many places. The huge change that has occurred in the last 20 years is that this information no longer exists in large rooms full of filing cabinets, but in a small room in a single computer. It would have taken many trucks to remove the personnel records of the State of California employees 20 years ago. A few years ago, the entire database was stolen by a computer hacker.

In sum, if we conceive of identity as composed primarily of information that is linked to a biological reference via an information system or specific technology, then it is possible to analyze the opportunity structure that makes it easy to steal this information and that reveals weaknesses in the process of authentication. Let us continue with the idea that "Hot products attract theft" (Clarke, 1999:2).

IDENTITY INFORMATION AS A "HOT PRODUCT"

The notion of "hot products" developed by Clarke (1999) demonstrates how particular products become more prone to theft than others. The attributes that such products have are described by the acronym CRAVED: the products are Concealable, Removable, Available, Valuable, Enjoyable and Disposable. Newman and Clarke (2003) have demonstrated the uncanny fit of information as a hot product to this model when applied to e-commerce crime. CRAVED information is:

Concealable. Thieves may have thought it easy to remove a magazine from a stand in a store and conceal it under their coats, but on the Internet one can steal information – including the personal information of others – without ever having personally to possess it, and can do so from halfway around the world.

Removable. The whole raison d'être of the Internet is that information is removable. In fact, it is constantly on the move. It is therefore intrinsically vulnerable to interception and deflection to places not originally intended. Files are removable and replicable countless times. Millions of individuals' identities are embedded in those files.

Available. Some argue that the true revolution of the Internet is that it has made *all* information potentially available to *everyone*. Personal information and records are there for the taking. In fact, one does not even have to steal them. One can buy identification information such as social security numbers cheaply, breed other identification documents from them, and then convert these into cash.

Valuable. In the information society, information is like money (actually, in the case of banks it *is* money). There is much information that has immediate value to criminals: credit card numbers, bank accounts, passwords and etc., which they can use to commit a wide variety of fraudulent crimes in someone else's name.

Enjoyable. Joyriding was a favorite delinquency when automobiles became all pervasive in the 20th century. The literature on hackers, who are often clever schoolboys (and sometimes mischievous adults), clearly demonstrates the joy they experience in overcoming the challenge of breaking into protected computer environments (Levy, 1984). For the identity thief, the rewards come when stolen identities are converted into cash or when they commit crimes in another person's name, easily escaping detection or punishment.

Durable. Usually, stolen items are called "hot" because continued possession of the stolen goods increases the risks of getting caught. In the case of the identity thief, the immediate disposal of the identity is not so pressing because the immediate chances of getting caught are slim.[4] Rather, the value of the stolen identity increases the longer it can be retained and reused. The time available to use an identity may stretch from days to years. It is a most durable hot product.

THE INTERNET: A PERFECT ENVIRONMENT FOR THEFT

A bank robber's dream would be a bank on a busy street that has a large vault in the back room, in which there are back doors as well as front access. There would be places on the same street where the robber could learn about the bank's routines, the exact locations of the doors to the vault, and even social gatherings with bank officials offering many opportunities to learn the combination to the vault. Best of all, he would become invisible and simply pass by the tellers, and sneak money from the till. Newman and Clarke (2003) argue that the Internet environment, which includes both hardware and software and in which much personal and business information resides, reproduces such a dream world for the thief. The characteristics of this dream world are summarized by the acronym SCAREM:

Stealth. The thieves, in fact anyone, can make themselves invisible on the Internet, a perfect condition for carrying out a crime (Denning and Baugh, 2000). Identity theft is a logical choice.

Challenge. The literature on hackers is replete with one primary motivation: to "beat" the computing system (Clough and Mungo, 1992). Taking on another's identity adds even more to the thrill of the crime.

Anonymity. Anonymity abounds on the Internet and it differs from Stealth, which is to be sneaky and secretive. Anonymity is a common way of doing business, just as when one pays for an item with cash in a retail store. There is also research evidence linking anonymity to deindividuation, a psychological condition that allows individuals to act irresponsibly or criminally (Wortley, 1997).

Reconnaissance. Perhaps the most important element in the choices that a criminal makes in carrying out a crime is the choice of a suitable target. The Internet makes it possible to scan thousands of Web servers and even millions of personal computers that are connected to the Web, looking for "holes" or gaps in security. Fraudsters can peddle their scams to millions of e-mail users for virtually no cost (though legislation has recently increased the penalties for spamming).

Escape. The crime-inducing aspects of the information system environment of anonymity, deception and stealth combine to make it extremely difficult for law enforcement to link the crime to the individual perpetrator, especially when the crime itself may never be detected, even by its victims (Ahuja, 1997).

Multiplicity. A traditional theft, such as a bank robbery, is a relatively finite act. However, if an offender hacks into a bank's files, this one crime can be multiplied exponentially, since it makes available to the offender a huge number of new opportunities to commit crime by exploiting access to the bank's accounts, which include personal and financial information.

SCAREM provides highly attractive opportunities to steal information. And the personal information that contributes to one's identity moves constantly through that SCAREM system. Thus, the opportunities available to offenders to commit identity theft are major factors that account for both the commission of the crime and its apparent[5] increase in recent years.

EXPLOITING OPPORTUNITIES: TECHNIQUES OF IDENTITY THEFT

Offenders have developed various techniques to exploit the information environment described above. The techniques used by identity thieves may be divided into roughly two categories: techniques they use to steal the identities, and techniques they use to convert these identities to advantage.[6]

How Offenders Steal Identities

Some of the notoriety of identity theft arose with media coverage of the dangers of buying and selling on the Internet. Until recently, Internet-related identity theft probably constituted a small proportion of all identity theft, less than 20%, though there are limited data to support this impression. Javelin Strategy & Research (Better Business Bureau, 2005) found that less than 5% of identity theft cases (in which the cause was known) occurred during online transactions; only 11.6% could be attributed to other forms of computer crime, including the use of spyware, computer viruses and computer hackers. Synovate (2003) notes that 13% of all victims' information was obtained through a transaction (Figure 1), including those via the Internet, but more research is needed to weed out Internet-related identity theft from other forms. However, there are many definitional problems here.

For example, just one act of hacking into a database may reap thousands of credit card numbers and other personal data. These may then be used to commit thousands of thefts offline. The high percentage in Figure 1 of victims reporting that they did not know how they lost their personal information suggests that the loss could have occurred via the Internet or other electronic means over which the victim has no control. However,

Figure 1: How Personal Information Is Obtained.

Source: Synovate (2003).[7]

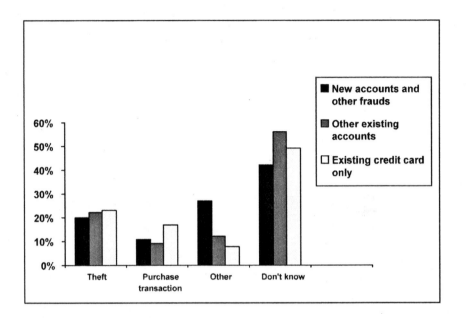

the ways offenders steal identities are primarily low-tech. Some methods are more popular than others, as is shown in Figures 1 and 2.

- They steal wallets or purses from shopping bags, from cars, or by pick-pocketing.

- They steal mail by several means. They may simply take it from insecure mailboxes, submit a false change-of-address form to the post office to direct someone's mail to themselves, or collude with a postal employee to steal mail that contains personal information. Mail that is useful to offenders includes pre-approved credit card applications, energy or telephone bills, bank or credit card statements, and convenience checks. In 2002, the U.S. Postal Inspection Service (USPIS) made 5,858 mail theft arrests. The first quarter of fiscal year 2004 saw 1,522 mail theft and identity theft arrests by the USPIS nationally (http://www.identity theft911.com/).

Figure 2: How Personal Information Is Obtained.

Source:: U.S. General Accounting Office (2002b: 27).[8]

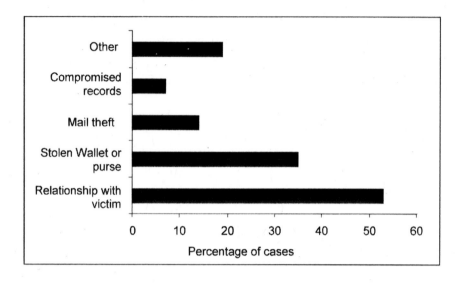

- They rummage through residential trash cans or through business dumpsters ("dumpster diving").

- They obtain people's credit reports by posing as someone who is legally permitted to do so, such as a landlord or employer.

- They collude with or bribe employees of businesses, government agencies, or service organizations, such as hospitals and health maintenance organizations (HMOs), to obtain personnel or client records, or if they are employees, they access the information themselves.

- They break into homes to find personal information on paper or on personal computers.

- They hack into corporate computers and steal customer and employee databases, then sell them on the black market or extort money for their return.

- They call credit card issuers and change the billing address for an account. The offender immediately runs up charges on the account, knowing that the victim will not receive the bill for some time, if ever.

- They buy identities on the street for the going rate (about $25), or buy credit cards that may be either counterfeit or stolen.

- They buy counterfeit documents such as birth certificates, visas, or passports. In 2001, the U.S. Immigration and Naturalization Service intercepted over 100,000 fraudulent passports, visas, alien registration cards, and entry permits (U.S. Government Accounting Office, 2002a; herein U.S. GAO).

- They buy false or counterfeit IDs on the Internet for as little as $50.

- They counterfeit checks and credit or debit cards, using another person's name. All the technology for reproducing plastic cards, including their holograms and magnetic strips, can be bought on the Internet (Newman and Clarke, 2003).

- They steal Personal Identification Numbers (PINs) and user IDs, using software available on the Internet; trick Internet users into giving their passwords and other personal information; or watch users punch in their PINs on telephones or at ATMs.

- They use a single stolen ID to obtain legitimate IDs they can use for a wide variety of additional frauds.

- They gain entry into ID-issuing agencies, such as motor vehicle departments, by using bribery or extortion, or posing as employees.

How Offenders Use Stolen Identities

- They open a new credit card account using the victim's name. All this requires, apart from the applicant's address, is a few pieces of information: the victim's mother's maiden name, the victim's birth date, and, sometimes, the victim's social security number.

- They open a landline or cell phone account in the victim's name.

- They open a bank account in the victim's name. They often open multiple accounts in multiple places, and write bad checks on each.

- They file for bankruptcy under the victim's name, to avoid paying their own debts or to avoid eviction.

- They steal the victim's identity, take over his or her insurance policies, and make false claims for "pain and suffering" suffered from auto accidents (Willox, 2000).

- They take out auto loans or mortgages under the victim's name and residence.

- They submit fraudulent tax returns using the victim's identity, and collect the refunds.

- They submit applications for social security using others' identities (often those of people who have died), and receive social security payments.

REDUCING OPPORTUNITY

Since identity theft is often composed of old crimes carried out in a new environment, it follows that many of the standard techniques of opportunity reduction should apply. Newman and Clarke (2003) have demonstrated how this approach may be applied to a range of computer-related crimes, especially e-commerce crimes. In addition, identity theft may be intertwined with traditional kinds of crimes that are used to obtain identity-related items, such as burglary of houses, muggings where a person's wallet is taken, or theft of personal items from cars. What follows is a brief outline of how the techniques of situational crime prevention may be applied to the prevention of identity theft per se. This attempt can only be tentative at this stage, since there is little or no research on the effectiveness of the techniques outlined below in preventing identity theft. However, all the basic techniques listed have been shown to work to some degree in prevention of theft of particular products and in particular environments.[9]

A difficulty in applying the techniques is that identity theft occurs in many different settings and is related to many different kinds of crimes, some of them quite specific, and may themselves be composed of specific behaviors, such as, for example, credit card fraud or mugging. Even with seemingly specific crimes such as check or card fraud, close analysis of these crimes reveals a highly complex opportunity structure and many different avenues that thieves take in carrying out those crimes (Newman, 2003; Mativat and Tremblay, 1997; Lacoste and Tremblay, 2003). Thus, the following outline of techniques can only be roughly indicative of what is possible. It should be read more as an outline of an entire program of research that is needed to establish effectiveness or refine techniques of intervention.

Techniques to Reduce Identity Theft

Situational prevention divides up the possible techniques into five categories:

1. Increase the effort the offender must make to complete the crime.

2. Increase the risks of getting caught.

3. Reduce the rewards that result from the crime.

4. Reduce provocations that may encourage or otherwise tempt offenders.

5. Remove excuses that offenders may use to justify their crime.

Table 1 summarizes the techniques as they may be applied to identity theft (see also the Berg and Willison chapters in this volume for additional applications of situational crime prevention to the problem of identity theft). While there are aspects of these five categories of techniques that clearly apply specifically to preventing identity theft, some appear much more relevant than others. Certainly the first three broad categories of increasing effort, increasing risks and reducing rewards appear most relevant, although it must be kept in mind that there are many different crimes involved in identity theft, in response to which there are a wide range of techniques available. For example, wallets may be stolen from cars. The techniques to prevent such crimes may depend on a whole range of matters to do with where the car is parked, whether it is locked, whether valuables are displayed inside the car and so on, all of which have little to do directly with the identity that is stolen by way of the wallet.

The role of technology in providing opportunities to offenders has been emphasized throughout this chapter. Table 1 reflects the heavy role of technology both in providing opportunities for offenders and also providing techniques to thwart them. If there are weaknesses in the information systems that make the exchange of information so easy in the marketplace, offenders will exploit those weaknesses. However, one cautionary note is in order. Information systems and technologies have one basic weakness: they require humans to manage them. And where humans are involved we expect there to be weakness. This fact of human nature (relative to machines) is very much a part of columns 3 through 5 of Table 1. So it is not surprising that almost all major break-ins of computing systems – where databases of personal information reside – have resulted

Table 1: Techniques to Reduce Identity Theft

Increase the Effort	Increase the Risks	Reduce the Rewards	Reduce Provocations	Remove Excuses
Target harden	*Extend guardianship*	*Conceal targets*	*Avoid disputes*	*Set rules*
• Tamper-proof documents and cards	• Close scrutiny, background checks of employees with access to ID databases	• No social security numbers on health, school cards	• Maintain positive management-employee relations	• Responsible computer use policy
• Firewalls		• No credit card numbers on receipts		*Post instructions in college dorms, workplace*
• Shred documents (paper and electronic) containing sensitive information	*Assist natural surveillance*	• Place ATMs so keystrokes cannot be observed or recorded	*Reduce arousal and temptation*	• "Respect Privacy"
	• ATMs in well lit areas	• Encryption	• Avoid public disclosure of security holes and patches in software	• "Protect our customers' privacy"
Control access to facilities	• Disallow employees to take work home	*Remove targets*	• Do not boast of security features in software	*Alert conscience*
• Lock areas with sensitive information (i.e., mail boxes, file rooms)	• Support whistleblowers (incentives for informal surveillance)	• Pre-paid cards for pay phones		• "Hacking hurts people"
• Card/password access to ID databases	*Reduce anonymity*	• Smart cards that contain limited personal ID information		*Assist compliance*
• ID for mail forwarding	• Photo, thumb print on ID documents, credit cards	• Do not leave wallets in cars (personal guardianship/prevention)		• Provide shredders for employees
• Disallow remote access to databases	• Require additional ID for online purchases	• Limit sale/sharing of personal information		
• Limit number of persons with access to ID databases	• Train clerks, police, officials in document authentication procedures	*Identify property*		
	Utilize place managers	• Guaranteed ID authentication services (e.g. Microsoft Passport)		
	• Reward vigilance for supervisors of employee/customer records	• Vehicle ID licensing and parts marking		

Table 1: *(continued)*

Increase the Effort	Increase the Risks	Reduce the Rewards	Reduce Provocations	Remove Excuses
Deflect offenders	*Strengthen formal surveillance*	*Disrupt markets*		
• Require several forms of ID to obtain new ID or replacement	• Retain backup files of computer usage	• Monitor pawn shops		
Control tools/weapons	• Track keystrokes of computer users	• Monitor retail returns departments		
• Control sale of ID making equipment (card readers, stripers, printers)	• Monitor all utilization of ID databases	• Monitor deliveries to vacant houses		
• Use tracking ID tags to track location of use and who uses machine	• Cameras on ATMs, at checkout counters, shipping and mailing services, ID granting agencies	• Monitor classified ads		
• Control pre-approved offers and applications for credit via mail	• Background checks of employees	• Monitor Internet sites and spam		
		Deny benefits		
		• Swift notification of stolen credit card		
		• Flag fraudulent transactions in real-time		

Source: Adapted from Newman and Clarke (2003).

– 23 –

from a dishonest employee who had access – or sold access to an outsider. So it is important to recognize that many situational techniques that may be relevant to reducing identity theft may be considerably "low-tech," directed at keeping employees honest. Any fantastic technological security system is only as dependable as the employees who manage it.

CONCLUSIONS AND CAVEAT: TECHNOLOGY AND THE "ARMS RACE"

Since the information systems of today are the outcome of the incessant march of technological innovation, it should come as no surprise that offenders will also take advantage of new technologies, often getting one step (or more) ahead of the inventors of these new technologies. Offenders were very quick, for example, to see that pay-as-you-go mobile phones were an excellent opportunity for theft of phones and phone services. The design of mobile phones clearly contributed to their theft in the United Kingdom (Harrington and Mayhew, 2002) and to their "cloning" and theft of cell phone service in the United States (Clarke et al., 2001). Similarly, no sooner had credit card manufacturers started to place holograms on credit cards, than counterfeiters obtained the very same machines and began to apply holograms too (Newman and Clarke, 2003). Researchers have termed this process an "arms race," echoing the language of neo-evolutionary theory (Ekblom, 1999; Pease, 2001).

While we are a long way from linking criminological theories to neo-evolutionary theory (although see Felson, 2005), the reference serves to impress on us the force with which technology drives the process of innovation and adaptation in the marketplace. Thus, emerging technologies and old technologies serve to provide signposts as to where or how identity thieves will strike next. Three facets of the technology environment help us in assessing the promise (both positive and negative) of technologies. These are:

1. *The specific technology and its design purpose.*
   In regard to identity theft, such technologies include:

   - Tamper-proofed plastic cards such as debit, check, credit, phone, college IDs, visas, driver's license, workplace IDs, and various kinds of "smart" cards.

   - Tamper-proofed documents such as visas, passports, birth and death certificates, letters of credit, documents of ownership, property titles, documents of financial exchange, wills, and etc.

- Firewalls and encryption software used for online transactions, such as online purchases by credit card; online voting, online renewal of motor vehicle registration etc.

- RFID chips (Remote Frequency ID chips) that allow for the tracking of people and objects. These chips, rapidly evolving, make it possible to track cattle, cars, people, and products. They are already quickly being incorporated by businesses to track inventory and sales, and parents may purchase knapsacks for their children that have RFIDs embedded in them for tracking their kids at school. Prescription drugs will now be tracked with RFID chips. The possibility that credit cards, mobile phones and other hot products could be embedded with such chips raises the prospect that possession of these "hot products" makes them really hot.

2. *The system within which the technology is applied or works, that is, the authentication procedures used to link the physical or electronic object to an individual.*

Procedures for authentication vary according to the technology and purpose of the ID. Most issuers of drivers' licenses have a system that requires the showing of additional documents of identification, although these vary considerably in stringency. However, the purchase of items, whether online or in a retail store, may receive only perfunctory authentication. Research has shown clearly that even the addition of elementary authentication requirements at checkout, such as a password or photograph ID, substantially reduces check or card fraud (Knutsson and Kulhorn, 1997). A significant research project therefore might review and develop model guidelines for the authentication procedures to be followed in (a) issuing all forms of ID, and (b) authenticating IDs at point of contact. This could be followed up by development of training guidelines for all individuals whose jobs require that they check IDs. This would range across many government agencies to almost all retail purchasing.

After the 9/11 terrorist attacks in the U.S., there was a call for national ID cards, since many of the 9/11 terrorists had easily stolen passports and obtained false driving licenses. It can be seen that if one's ID were encapsulated in just one object, a national ID, this could make the work of the identity thief much easier, since he/she would only have to steal one object, rather than having to breed other forms of identification. However, others have argued that new technologies available for "smart cards" could in fact make a universal ID possible, since such cards may be programmed to contain different levels of security, providing access only to particular personal information depending on the specific task at hand. For example, a retail purchase may not require knowing the cardholder's date of birth, but getting a driving license would.

Another argument in favor of smart cards is that they can be constructed in such a way that they can contain all the data necessary for carrying out most transactions, so that massive databases containing all cardholders' personal information are not needed (for a review of these issues, see Newman and Clarke, 2003). While the introduction of national ID cards is a highly charged political issue, research nevertheless should be conducted to evaluate smart cards and to work out ways of introducing them into the marketplace along with other technologies. It should be emphasized, however, that offenders will quickly overcome the embedded security designed into these cards and that this is a constantly evolving process. Thus, the authentication procedures are just as important as the technology, so research must take account of this.

3. *The infrastructure that supports both of the above, that is, the assembly of databases that contain the information that is embedded in the technologies and systems (i.e. personal information).*

    All of the technologies and systems above depend on the collection, storage and quick access to the personal information that is linked to the IDs, whether electronic, paper or plastic. While technologies of various kinds can protect these databases, the fact that they must be accessed constantly for the verification of individual IDs means that they are open to attack. However, as reported above, access to such databases has, with some notable exceptions, been by low-tech means, by disgruntled or otherwise motivated employees who have access to the databases. Thus, the system of maintaining, accessing and preserving these databases depends for its security in the long run on the individuals who maintain them. This is not to say that technology cannot help reduce this risk. The introduction of electronic verification of credit card accounts at point of sale, for example, eliminated one significant security risk: the checkout clerk who previously had the discretion to decide whether or not to check the purchaser's credit card with the list of stolen card numbers. This practice made it impossible for clerks either to be negligent in checking the authenticity of the card account or to collude with purchasers.

One final issue is worth consideration. It is difficult to escape the conclusion that some businesses see the crime of identity theft as a business opportunity. They have swamped the mass media with advertisements to scare consumers into purchasing shredders, or purchasing insurance riders to their household insurance to protect them against identity theft. Some card issuers have marketed special check cashing cards or special credit cards bearing the photograph of the cardholder. Card issuers generally do not charge customers for these special cards, but do use them as a marketing tool to break into new markets. Of the businesses involved in these various enterprises, insurance companies are probably the major players that should be engaged in any attempt to introduce improved security for identities. It is the insurance companies, after all, whose ancient business model is premised on the assumption that consumers will pay money to ensure the security of themselves and their possessions. The complex interrelationship between businesses and the opportunities afforded for crime, including identity theft, requires much further investigation. It boils down to one significant question: Who should pay for crime?

Address correspondence to: grn92@albany.edu

NOTES

1. We could push the analogy further by observing that cars have their own identities, which can also be stolen, and indeed are by thieves who find that stealing cars in the old fashioned way is much more difficult now that there has been significant improvement in car security. See: Maxfield and Clarke (2004).

2. Yet this modern idea of identity sits on the paradox of anonymity (i.e., keeping one's identity secret), which for centuries has been a cornerstone of the trust required in the marketplace for the exchange of goods and services (Newman and Clarke, 2003; Seabright, 2004) – and in democracies regarding the guarantee of being able to vote for one's candidate without fear of reprisal. At the same time, it has been necessary for almost all societies on this planet to develop complex procedures to collect detailed information about every individual

(Marx, 2001; Newman and Clarke, 2003). This information is needed for the basic functioning of modern life, such as finding friends, mailing a letter, collecting taxes, and keeping track of one's money. It is this paradox that makes authenticating identities so difficult, particularly in "open societies" (Jones and Levi, 2000), although the rapidly rising use of credit cards in payment for goods and services – now the major form of payment for goods and services in the U.S. – suggests that anonymity in the market place is rapidly disappearing even though it is a cherished value of all democracies. It may be that the convenience in everyday life offered by credit cards and other service products in the marketplace is simply too good to have, and in the long run it renders the values of privacy and anonymity as irrelevant, regardless of the powerful ethical, moral and political arguments.

3. One could take this further and suggest that the ultimate identity theft occurs in certain religions when an individual is occupied by a demon that steals or takes over the identity of the individual.

4. Different parts of identity information may vary in "hotness." Account numbers are hot (in the sense of dangerous) because they can be changed and are likely to be detected earlier. Social security numbers are "cold" because their misuse can continue even after the misuse has been detected but hot (in the sense of being desirable) because of this. The value of a stolen identity also decreases as the victim's resources are depleted or their credit limit is approached.

5. There are many reasons why it is not possible to state definitively that identity theft has in fact increased either recently or over a considerable period. See McNally (2008).

6. It should be noted that, except where indicated, these lists of techniques are derived from data taken mostly from Internet sources of varying kinds. These include newspaper and magazine reports, media interviews with fraud investigators and law enforcement personnel, and information provided on various advocacy Web sites seeking to either help victims or to sell services designed to prevent victimization by identity theft. There have been few formal studies of identity thieves' practices or techniques that have conducted interviews or observations directly with the thieves. The exceptions to this general observation are the studies on check and credit card fraud by Mativat and Tremblay (1997) and Lacoste and Tremblay (2003), and also the chapter by Copes and Vieraitis in this volume.

7. *Theft*: Nearly a quarter of all victims who knew how their information was obtained reported that their information had been lost or stolen:

14% of all victims reported that their wallet, checkbook or credit card had been lost or stolen; 4% of all victims cited stolen mail as the source of their information. *Purchase transaction*: 13% of all victims who knew how their information was obtained reported that their information had been taken during a transaction, either through the credit card receipt or through a purchase made via Internet, mail or phone. *"Other"*: 14% of all victims who knew how their information was obtained reported some "other" type of means, including people who had access to the information such as a relative or co-worker, or individuals who had been given the information and later used it for some other purpose.

8. This graph represents only those victims who knew and reported how their information was stolen. This constitutes 20.5% of all victims who complained to the FTC during the period covered (1999–2001). One victim may report that multiple methods were used. The Better Business Bureau website (2005) contains a similar, but more detailed graph for a 2004 study conducted by Javelin Strategy & Research.

9. These are generally reviewed in Clarke (1997). Many of the techniques are also reviewed and tested in the various volumes of *Crime Prevention Studies*.

REFERENCES

Ahuja, V. (1997). *Secure commerce on the Internet.* New York, NY: Academic Press.

Better Business Bureau (2005, January 26). *New research shows that identity theft is more prevalent offline with paper than online.* Available at: http://www.bbbonline.org/idtheft/safetyQuiz.asp

Clarke, R.V. (1997). *Situational crime prevention: Successful case studies,* 2nd ed. Monsey, NY: Criminal Justice Press.

——— (1999). *Hot products. Understanding, anticipating and reducing the demand for stolen goods.* Police Research Series, Paper 98. London, UK: Home Office.

Clarke, R.V., R. Kemper and L. Wyckoff (2001). "Controlling cell phone fraud in the US: Lessons for the UK '*Foresight*' Prevention Initiative." *Security Journal* 14(1): 7-22.

Clough, B. and P. Mungo (1992). *Approaching zero: Data crime and the computer underworld.* London, UK: Faber and Faber.

Denning, D.E. and W.E. Baugh, Jr. (2000). "Hiding crimes in cyberspace." In D. Thomas and B. Loader (Eds.), *Cybercrime* (pp. 105-131). London, UK: Routledge. Available at: http://www.cs.georgetown.edu/~denning/crypto/hiding1.doc

Ekblom, P. (1999). "Can we make crime prevention adaptive by learning from other evolutionary struggles?" *Studies on Crime and Crime Prevention,* 8(1): 27-51.

Felson, M. (2005). *Crime and nature*. Thousand Oaks, CA: Sage.

Harrington, V. and P. Mayhew (2002). *Mobile phone theft*. Home Office Research Study 235. London, UK: Home Office.

Home Office (2004). *The British Crime Survey. Patterns of crime*. Available at: http://www.homeoffice.gov.uk/rds/patterns1.html

Jones, G. and M. Levi (2000). "The value of identity and the need for authenticity." Research Paper, *Turning the Corner: Crime 2020*. Available at: http://www.foresight.gov.uk/Previous_Rounds/Foresight_1999__2002/Crime_Prevention/Reports/Turning%20the%20Corner/essay5.htm

Knutsson, J., and E. Kulhorn (1997). "Macromeasures Against Crime: The Example of Check Forgeries." In R.V. Clarke (ed.), *Situational crime prevention: Successful case studies*, 2nd ed. Monsey, NY: Criminal Justice Press.

Lacoste, J., and P. Tremblay (2003). "Crime innovation: A script analysis of patterns in check forgery." In M.J. Smith and D.B. Cornish (Eds.), *Theory for Practice for Situational Crime Prevention*. (Crime Prevention Studies, vol. 16, pp. 171-198.) Monsey, NY: Criminal Justice Press.

Levy, S. (1984). *Hackers: Heroes of the computer revolution*. New York, NY: Bantam/Doubleday.

Marx, G.T. (2001). "Identity and anonymity: Some conceptual distinctions and issues for research." In J. Caplan and J. Torpey (Eds.), *Documenting Individual Identity*, (pp. 311-327). Princeton, NJ: Princeton University Press.

Mativat, F., and P. Tremblay (1997). "Counterfeiting credit cards: Displacement effects, suitable offenders, and crime wave patterns." *British Journal of Criminology* 37(2): 165-183.

Maxfield, M., and R. Clarke (Eds.), (2004). *Understanding and Preventing Auto Theft. Crime Prevention Studies*, vol. 17. Monsey, NY: Criminal Justice Press.

McNally, M.M. (2008). *Trial by circumstance: Is identity theft a modern-day moral panic?* Unpublished Ph.D. dissertation, Rutgers University.

Newman, G.R. (2003). *Check and card fraud*. Problem Oriented Guides for Police No. 21. Washington, D.C. U.S. Department of Justice, COPS and Center for Problem Oriented Policing. Available at: http://www.popcenter.org/Problems/problem-check-card-fraud.htm

Newman, G.R. and R.V. Clarke (2003). *Superhighway robbery: Preventing e-commerce crime*. London, UK: Willan.

Pease, K. (2001). *Cracking crime through design*. London, UK: Design Council.

Seabright, P. (2004) *The company of strangers*. Princeton, NJ: Princeton University Press.

Synovate (2003). *Federal Trade Commission – Identity Theft Survey Report*. Available at: http://www.ftc.gov/os/2003/09/synovatereport.pdf

"The decline of the English burglary." (2004, May 27). *The Economist*.

U.S. General Accounting Office (2002a, June 25). *Identity fraud: Prevalence and links to alien illegal activities*. Before the Subcommittee on Crime, Terrorism and Homeland Security and the Subcommittee on Immigration, Border Security, and Claims, Committee on the Judiciary, House of Representatives. Available at: http://www.consumer.gov/idtheft/reports/gao-d02830t.pdf

U.S. General Accounting Office (2002b, March). *Identity theft: Prevalence and cost appear to be growing*. Report to Congressional requesters. Available at: http://www.gao.gov/new.items/d02363.pdf

Willox, N. (2000). *Identity theft: Authentication as a solution*. National Fraud Center (www.fraud.org), Identity Theft Summit, March 15-16.

Wortley, R. (1997). "Reconsidering the role of opportunity in situational crime prevention." In G. Newman, R.V. Clarke and S.G. Shoham (Eds.). *Rational Choice and Situational Crime Prevention* (pp. 65-81). Aldershot, UK: Ashgate.

CHARTING THE CONCEPTUAL LANDSCAPE OF IDENTITY THEFT

by

Megan M. McNally
School of Criminal Justice
Rutgers University, Newark

Abstract: *This chapter explores the conceptual and procedural complexities surrounding the issue of identity theft. The discussion begins by outlining a universal script for the commission and consequences of this offense. This script consists of three main scenes: the acquisition of personal information (Time 1), the misuse of personal information (Time 2), and the outcomes of victimization (Time 3). The meaning and mechanics of identity theft are then deconstructed through an analogy to the story of Goldilocks and the Three Bears, which is also useful for illustrating the multiple and repeated dimensions of identity theft victimization. Finally, the contours of identity theft are mapped onto this universal script, with a particular focus on highlighting the range of opportunities available for research and prevention. Considering the current shortage of detailed data regarding identity theft, this exercise can be useful for structuring extant information and fine-tuning data-collection instruments. Further development of this identity theft script will additionally help to accomplish the goals of situational crime prevention.*

The topic of identity theft is largely uncharted territory in the modern world. Although a number of entities have staked a claim in this area over the past decade, each has a somewhat different view with regard to what it is and what should be done about it. Considering the dimensions of this problem, all parties are aware that an effective response will entail cooperation and better information; yet those involved in this effort still seem to be guided by separate maps of the subject. Despite divergent terminologies and interests, however, there is a shared conceptual terrain underlying the events collectively known as identity theft. While a good portion of this landscape is revealed through deduction, there are a few densely populated regions that require more analytical attention. As such, the current chapter attempts to sketch out the contours of this offense in the hope of moving forward together towards its prevention.

This exercise begins by outlining a broad map or script (Cornish, 1994) of the event sequence underlying the commission of identity theft. Similar to a theatrical script, a crime script is a heuristic device that can be used to situate the interactions of actors and props across space and over time. While scripts can be constructed at various levels of abstraction, intricate scripts are best suited for the goals of situational crime prevention. Given that most identity theft data comes from victimization surveys, however, we know relatively little about the processes underlying offending itself. Consequently, the dynamics of identity theft are traced at varying levels of detail in order to highlight the different forms of this offense and illustrate the range of opportunities available for research and prevention (for another example of the script approach, see the Willison chapter in this volume). An analogy to the story of Goldilocks and the Three Bears also provides a familiar set of imagery for uncovering and introducing the foundations of identity theft. While this discussion is intentionally far reaching at times, examining both the forest and the trees of identity theft, its purpose is to translate what we already know into a language that everyone can understand. What follows is therefore a conceptual exploration of identity theft: a very old tale about privacy and victimization with a modern twist (and a few bears).

THE IDENTITY THEFT SCRIPT

Contemporary stories about identity theft are all variations on a single theme: the misuse of someone's personal information (or identity) to facilitate fraud. Apart from the range of activities encapsulated by this description, these stories also share a fundamental progression of events, as shown in Figure 1. Each of these stages or scenes (Time 1, Time 2, Time 3)

Figure 1: The Scenes of Identity Theft.

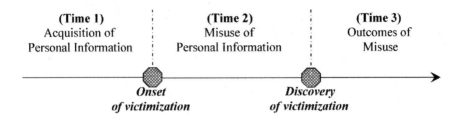

contains very different opportunities for offending and prevention, but all are linked within the temporal framework of this generalized script. First, personal information is obtained and subsequently compromised (often repeatedly). A victim then discovers the misuse and has a chance to respond. An offender's path will eventually end in either capture or desistance, but his or her activities may continue well past the point of discovery.

Given its simplicity, the utility of this script is limited to marking the procedural boundaries of this offense over time. Prior to delving into what each scene entails, however, this identity theft script will be equated to a well-known story with the same moral tenor. The tale of Goldilocks and the Three Bears has been told in countless ways over the past century, but this story can be expressed in basic criminological terms: a youth unlawfully enters a residence (Onset), commits acts that ostensibly result in criminal harm (Time 2), and is caught red-handed (Discovery). Like most classic fairy tales and bedtime stories, the story of Goldilocks also contains a lesson for children. The general message of this particular story is identical to that of identity theft in that they both pertain to invading the privacy of others, but there are other similarities between them that can be helpful for visualizing the meaning and the mechanics of identity theft.[1]

SCRIPTING THE STORY OF IDENTITY THEFT

In the identity theft version of this story, the character of Goldilocks (i.e., the identity thief) has been portrayed as devious and versatile, but very little information is actually available. Considering further the lingering idea that anyone can be an offender, then why not a young girl with golden hair? She may even be a he, or "Goldilocks" might simply represent another assumed identity – either real (i.e., the actual Goldilocks) or fictitious (e.g., a screen name). In terms of the basic opportunities available for committing identity theft, each is also represented among the members of the Bear family. Although this version of the story is different from the fairy tale because it places more emphasis on Goldilocks's adventures in the forest (Time 1) and the reaction of the Bears to their victimization (Time 3), her exploits inside their home (Time 2) epitomize the commission of identity theft.

Scene 1 (Time 1): The Acquisition of Personal Information

The story of identity theft begins in a forest where *personal information* literally grows on trees – aside from what is freely available for the taking, it can also be thrown away, given away, lost, stolen or sold. Before venturing any further, however, this pivotal identity theft character must be properly introduced. "Personal information," like "identity theft," has come to represent everything *and* the color of your kitchen sink. As such, the importance of distinguishing *between* different types of information is often overlooked. While it is generally understood that the social security number is the Holy Grail of identity theft, the largest victimization studies to date have focused on *how* information is obtained – not *what* is obtained, and both are important considerations.[2]

Information can be physical or virtual; a social security card and a social security number cannot always be obtained or misused in the same ways, even though both provide access to the same information. A counterfeit card can be manufactured or other documents can be bred with a social security number, but this may require more skill than the average offender possesses and more effort than is perhaps necessary in most cases. A valid social security number can also be used without reference to the correct individual, and more attention should be focused on how and why this occurs.[3]

At the same time, the extent of damage that can be caused by any given piece of personal information other than a social security number is unclear. Most personal information commonly available to the public, such as that contained in a phone book, doesn't appear to pose much of a threat on its own. In the correct combination, however, mundane information holds considerably more power. Without a physical credit card, for example, an offender will likely need several different types of information to place fraudulent charges on an account (e.g., the account number, expiration date, security code, and the legitimate account holder's name, address or telephone number). The ultimate success of an offender therefore depends upon being able to meet the requirements for identification and authentication, which vary according to the type of activity attempted.

While pieces of personal information are akin to the keys of someone's social existence, only a skeleton key (like the social security number) can open every door; the opportunities that lie behind those doors are another matter. If an offender is able to breach or gain control over a victim's existing account directly with the card-issuing company, for example, s/he may obtain access to more important pieces of personal information, such as the individual's social security number. Some pieces of sensitive information are also relatively easy to change (e.g., a credit card number), while a social security number will never expire. To summarize the point more generally: personal information is not created, consumed or even compromised equally. Not every piece of misappropriated information can or will be misused, and not all misuse will result in criminal harm. Protecting sensitive pieces of personal information (e.g., account numbers, passwords, social security numbers) is nevertheless critical, as this is still the first line of defense against identity theft; that is, offenders cannot misuse what they do not have.[4]

Back on the forest path, Goldilocks is busy gathering the tools of her trade and her activities in this regard are not only dependent upon the opportunities that cross her path, but on her ability and willingness to capitalize upon them; in other words, her own level of motivation in terms of *taking* or *making* opportunities (Weisburd et al., 2001). An offender's motivation is important in another respect, for as the Bears will soon discover, not all forms of victimization are the same. While personal information is used instrumentally to obtain something of value, identity theft can also be wielded expressively as a form of revenge. Information is always an intermediate target (you can't commit identity theft without it); but the distal target (i.e., money, goods, services, employment, criminal anonymity, an ex-spouse) potentially impacts the manner in which each storyline plays out.

Although several variables interact to affect the opportunities available for obtaining personal information, there are only a few paths that can actually be trodden. The first is directly from the individual victim or his/her environment (e.g., residence, car), the second is directly from an information guardian or its environment (e.g., store, office), and the third is during a transaction (physical or otherwise) between the victim and the guardian. Once an offender has initially obtained some sensitive piece of personal information, however, s/he becomes a type of illegitimate guardian who may further sell or share this commodity.

Most of the methods used to obtain personal information (e.g., mail theft, dishonesty, hacking) are similar regardless of the pathway, but some may only be related to the specific opportunities along each. In particular, a distinction can be made between traditional and technology-based methods for obtaining personal information, but the role of either is currently unclear considering that many victims – approximately 51% (Synovate, 2003:30) – simply do not know how the offender acquired their information. Another vital consideration is the nature of the relationships between individuals, guardians and offenders because these will in some ways alter the opportunities that are available. These three main paths nevertheless represent a different point of origin and a different type of responsibility with regard to the protection of personal information.

Guardians and victims may play an active or passive role in this process. Guardians may negligently sell, share or lose personal information, but they may also be victims themselves (e.g., as the result of a database breach, or when an employee uses his or her position to illicitly acquire information). Individuals may be similarly victimized (i.e., robbed of their information) or negligent in a variety of ways, just as the Bears in one version of the story contributed to their own victimization by leaving the door unlocked. The controversy surrounding industry control over personal information has nevertheless been overshadowed by a continued emphasis on individual prevention (and a subsequent deluge of consumer ID theft-prevention products). While some research has focused on the risk of identity theft following a data breach (e.g., ID Analytics, 2005b, 2006),[5] more balanced attention needs to be given to this issue as a whole.

Although more detailed data is required to script the dynamic processes that might occur during Time 1, Table 1 provides an outline of its related elements as previously described. The first four rows ("Necessary Sequences") represent the minimum actions necessary to obtain personal information, and provide examples of the more specific scripting tracks that might be used. The order of these steps, however, is not necessarily fixed. An offender may be motivated to seek out personal information or may stumble upon an opportunity that entices him or her to misuse certain information. Depending upon the method that is used, actions related to

Table 1: Scripting the Acquisition of Personal Information (Time 1)

STAGES	TRACKS
NECESSARY SEQUENCES	
Identify Distal Target (Motivation)	Money, Goods, Services, Employment, Anonymity, Revenge
Locate Proximate Target (Personal Information)	Individual (e.g., person, personal computer)
	Transaction (e.g., person-to-person, over the Internet)
	Licit Guardian (e.g., dumpster, database)
	Illicit Guardian (e.g., dishonest employee, phisher)
Acquire Proximate Target (Method)	Traditional (e.g., lost/stolen wallet)
	Technology-based (e.g., hacking)
Avoid Detection	Successful (i.e., information obtained)
	Unsuccessful (i.e., diverted)
POSSIBLE SEQUENCES	
Alteration	Breeding
	Counterfeiting
	Splicing (hybrid identities)
Additional Targets	Sensitive Information (e.g., passwords)
	Mundane Information (e.g., date of birth)
Bypassing Controls	Traditional (e.g., lock)
	Technology-based (e.g., firewall)
ACTORS	
Co-Offenders	Formal Organization (e.g., syndicate)
	Informal Organization (e.g., acquaintances)
Individuals/Guardians	Unaware of Attempt/Misappropriation
	Aware & Respond
	Aware & Don't Respond
PROPS	
Information (original form)	Physical by Type (e.g., social security card)
	Virtual by Type (e.g., social security number)
Tools	Traditional (e.g., firearm)
	Technology-based (e.g., computer)

avoiding detection might also occur while acquiring the target and/or after it has been obtained. Many of these tracks can be broken down further into sub-tracks. Obtaining personal information from an individual, for example, could be scripted as a direct route from the victim (e.g., robbery, burglary, transferred willingly) or an indirect one (e.g., dumpster diving, lost wallet). Taken together, however, these stages reflect a motivated offender with a suitable target who is ultimately successful in acquiring the personal information necessary to commit identity theft.[6]

The next three rows in Table 1 ("Possible Sequences") represent activities that an offender might also be engaged in during Time 1, but the extent to which they occur – or the precise conditions under which they must occur – are unknown. Before personal information can be obtained, various types of situational controls may have to be diffused by an offender. Once it has been obtained, personal information may also have to be transformed before it can be misused, or additional information may be necessary. As the next two columns show, however, other actors (individuals, guardians, or co-offenders) may be involved in any of these sequences, whether necessary or possible for the acquisition of personal information. Searching for co-offenders, for example, may be a process in itself (Tremblay, 1993). Individuals or guardians may further be aware that the information has been wrongfully acquired, thus potentially rendering the target "hot" if any action is taken to prevent its misuse. The final two rows ("Props") illustrate the need to consider the form (i.e., physical or virtual) and type (e.g., account number or social security number) of information that is initially obtained, and the possibility that other tools may be involved at various points in these sequences (e.g., obtaining or altering information).

Over all, there are a number of potential patterns underlying this first scene of identity theft that are more complicated than the idea of a single offender taking a single piece of information from a single location. Some attempt should be made, therefore, to collect data sufficient for studying these processes in more detail, as well as the spatial and temporal aspects related to the misappropriation of personal information. While the stages and tracks outlined in Table 1 are not an exhaustive list, they are suggested as initial points of departure for scripting the dynamics involved at Time 1. Available data can also be used to begin this process, but more comprehensive data will be necessary for developing these elements and pathways further. As we return to the identity thief of this story, however, Goldilocks has somehow gained possession of the Bears' personal information.

Event: The Onset of Victimization

In Figure 1, the "onset of victimization" represents the initial transfer of personal information to facilitate an act of fraud. Despite differences in the processes culminating at this point, an offender's decision to misuse any type of personal information is the same because it will ultimately affect a particular individual. This is therefore the moment when identity theft victims are truly made; that is, the harms normally associated with this offense don't occur until *after* someone's personal information has been misused.[7] It should be acknowledged, however, that the act of obtaining personal information itself is sometimes considered to be identity theft. Javelin Strategy & Research (2007), for example, defines *identity theft* as the unauthorized access to personal information (Time 1) and *identity fraud* as its misuse (Time 2). Several U.S. jurisdictions have also criminalized identity theft to include the possession of personal information with the intent to commit fraud, which obviously occurs during Time 1. Although this distinction is conceptually important for a number of reasons, particularly when trying to decipher information about the topic, it has no effect on the processual dynamics involved.

Preventing the misuse of personal information after it has been obtained is the second line of defense against identity theft, and the methods for doing so largely lie in the proprietary realm of authentication. Identity theft offenders may also be diverted from completing the transfer of personal information at different times or locations, and research should be concerned with these points of deflection as they may offer insights for prevention. If offenders cannot be waylaid before their attempt to misuse personal information, the onus of prevention falls on those in charge of verifying that the offender is indeed the individual s/he is claiming to be. Even with these caveats in mind, however, the crux of what is popularly and collectively known as identity theft occurs inside the Bear family residence.

Scene 2 (Time 2): The Misuse of Personal Information

Goldilocks symbolically commits identity theft when she enters the home of the three Bears, or when she first presents their information as her own, but the similarities between different types of victimization largely end at the front door. In the classic version of events, Goldilocks starts her spree by targeting the porridge and then moves on to the chairs and the beds. The story of identity theft is similar in that a variety of activities are usually committed, and each victim is differentially affected. As opposed to telling this story from the offender's perspective, however, each of the Bears (Papa Bear, Mama Bear, and Baby Bear) will be used to represent a distinct type of victimization. This continuum of identity theft victimization is depicted in Figure 2, and each character will be considered in turn.

Figure 2: The Continuum of Identity Theft Victimization.

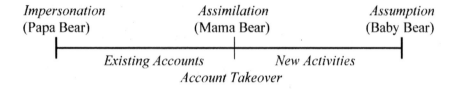

Impersonation   *Assimilation*   *Assumption*
(Papa Bear)   (Mama Bear)   (Baby Bear)

Existing Accounts   *New Activities*
Account Takeover

Papa Bear (Impersonation): Existing-Account Fraud

Existing-account fraud is the "Papa Bear" of identity theft. Visually speaking, he is the largest character in the tale, representing almost two-thirds of all identity theft victims. His victimization nevertheless results in the least amount of harm: his porridge was "too hot" to eat, and it was "too hard" to get comfortable on his furniture. This is the essence of existing-account misuse, regardless of the specific type of account that is affected (e.g., credit, bank, insurance). Personal information that enables someone to access an existing account (e.g., an account number, plastic card or password) is potentially the *hottest* type around, which makes prolonged misuse relatively difficult. Since this type of information can normally be changed at the request of an account holder, the victim's identity is more "borrowed" than "stolen," just as impersonation is a temporary form of character representation. The consequences associated with existing-account misuse vary according to the type of account that is involved, however, as will be illustrated in the final scene of identity theft (Time 3). To say that all forms of existing-account misuse are the same is nevertheless analogous to saying that all types of identity theft are the same. This broad distinction is still a useful contrast against the type of victimization experienced by Baby Bear.

Mama Bear (Assimilation): Account Takeover

The victimization of Mama Bear represents the midway point between the two main forms of identity theft (i.e., existing accounts and new activities).

Although takeover involves an existing account, control has been wrestled away from the individual who owns it; this part of the victim's identity has therefore been assimilated[8] for the offender's exclusive use. Takeover is the worst-case scenario of existing-account fraud, and even though it more closely resembles assumption in some respects, it is generally less serious than true-name fraud (i.e., new activities). Once a victim's status as the owner of an account has been altered, the processes for offending become *colder* than those involved with impersonation. While account takeover would seem to buy an offender some additional time at the outset, however, the opportunities for maintaining control in the long-term are unclear. In particular, the furniture in this house is "too soft," so offenders seemingly can't get too comfortable: a commandeered resource may eventually be depleted and the victim is likely to be close on their trail.

Baby Bear (Assumption): New Activities and Other Fraud

By all accounts, the opportunities available for victimizing Baby Bear are "just right." He is the smallest character, representing approximately one-third of all identity theft victims, but he also experiences a disproportionate amount of harm: his porridge is gone, his chair is broken, and the offender is literally discovered asleep in his bed. This is the epitome of identity theft, sometimes called "true-name fraud," in which an offender assumes the victim's identity to lead a sort of parallel existence. This category of activities is much more varied, but none are particularly likely to be discovered in a timely fashion, and this in turn affects the type and amount of damage that can result. This form of victimization would also seem to be most closely associated with social security number misuse, but non-financial activities (e.g., providing "stolen" information to legal authorities [criminal record fraud]) can occur as well.

Over all, this portrayal of identity theft victimization is not dissimilar to the one used by most research, which typically has two categories of "existing-account" misuse (credit card and non-credit card accounts) and the category of "new activities."[9] The problems associated with calling all of the Bears "identity theft victims" nevertheless remain. While it is necessary to disaggregate these categories for any purpose related to identity theft research or prevention, this initially wider reorganization is useful for mapping out these two conceptually distinct avenues for victimization (i.e., existing and new activities). Another immediate benefit to this approach relates to the issues of multiple and repeated victimization: "multiple" in the sense that more than one type of activity may be occurring, and "repeated" in the sense that any given activity may be occurring more than once.

The Multiple and Repeated Aspects of Identity Theft Victimization

The occurrence of identity theft is not neatly ordered into any of the categories described above because many victims experience more than one type of activity. According to the Federal Trade Commission's survey, for example, 65% of victims who experienced new-activities fraud also experienced some form of existing-account fraud; 40% who experienced the misuse of an existing non-credit card account also experienced the misuse of an existing credit card account (Synovate, 2003:5). This dimension of victimization is outlined in Table 2 in order to illustrate the associations between existing-account fraud (Papa Bear) and new-activities fraud (Baby Bear). Even these categories, however, must be further disaggregated into their constituent parts.

Table 2: Multiple Identity Theft Victimizations by Type

	Single Type of Victimization		Two or More Types of Victimization		Total
Existing Accounts (Papa Bear)	Credit Card Non-Credit Card	6% 1.2%	Credit Card & Non-Credit Card	.8%	**8%**
New Accounts or Activities (Baby Bear)	True-name Fraud	1.75%	True Name & Credit Card	1%	**4.7%**
			True Name & Non-Credit Card	1.2%	
			True Name, Credit Card & Non-Credit Card	.75%	
Total		**8.95%**		**3.75%**	**12.7%**

Source: Calculations for this table are based on information provided by Synovate (2003:5) for all identity theft victims (n=515) identified over a five-year period within the entire sample of respondents (N=4,057).

Existing-account fraud, for example, is represented in Table 2 as "credit card" and "non-credit card" fraud, but the latter consists of very different types of accounts (e.g., bank, Internet, insurance, telephone, utilities, etc.). The category of true-name fraud represents an even more varied assortment of events: new accounts (of any type), criminal record fraud, or receiving another type of benefit not readily classifiable as an "account" (e.g., housing, welfare, or employment). While it is important to tease out these distinctions for the purposes of crime prevention, Table 2 illustrates the uneven distribution of victims across these two main forms of victimization, thus confirming the size differential visually represented by the characters of Papa Bear and Baby Bear.

Papa Bear represents two types of existing-account fraud in Table 2 (credit card and non-credit card), but credit card fraud alone (6%) is responsible for almost half of the overall total (12.7%). Some forms of existing non-credit card account misuse (e.g., bank fraud) are generally more serious than their extant counterparts (e.g., credit card fraud) in terms of harm and reclamation, but they can also occur in combination with other types of fraud. The entire Papa Bear row (8%), however, comprises the majority of identity theft victimizations (12.7%). If this total were converted to represent 100% of all victims, existing-account fraud (of any type) would account for approximately 63% of all victims identified over a five-year period between 1998 and 2003; 16% of victims who experienced the misuse of an existing credit card account also experienced an attempted account takeover (Mama Bear). In short, existing-account fraud is a potentially mountainous problem in terms of its size but more of a molehill in terms of its harm.

In Table 2, new activities are represented as true-name fraud, in contrast to the two forms of existing-account misuse already described. As mentioned, however, Baby Bear's victimization is more of a mixed bag: that is, several different types of activities comprise this category. Nevertheless, 1.75% of the victims in this row only experienced some form of true-name fraud, while the other 2.95% of victims also experienced some type of existing-account fraud. Although victims who experience both types of misuse (i.e., existing and new) may actually have more opportunities to discover and respond to their victimization, this distinction is extremely important for understanding the common trails that might link different tracks of victimization together. In other words, it is important to understand whether existing-account fraud provides the tools necessary to commit true-name fraud, or whether the reverse is true (or both).

True-name fraud is unquestionably the most serious form of identity theft victimization in terms of its consequences, even though the activities involved and their resultant harms can vary widely. Baby Bear may therefore be the smallest of the victims, but as the final scene will show, his life is generally left in shambles.

The content of Table 2 also hints at some of the additional complexities related to the multiple and repeated aspects of identity theft victimization. Individuals may be victimized by different types of true-name fraud (e.g., a new account opened and a traffic ticket racked up in their name), or may be repeatedly victimized by the same type of activity (e.g., several new credit card accounts are opened). Several offenders may be involved in the victimization of a single individual, or a single offender may victimize several individuals. Entities in receipt of "stolen" personal information (e.g., financial institutions, governments) are further victimized alongside individuals. These activities might also be taking place in very different locations, and almost simultaneously.

Considering all of the dimensions that must be integrated into this scene of the script, Table 3 reflects only one necessary sequence for the commission of identity theft: the fraudulent transfer of personal information. While the initial transfer represents the onset of victimization, information may thereafter be transferred repeatedly and for very different purposes (represented as x^n in Table 3). Table 3 can also be extended to include the necessary sequences outlined in Table 1, although these descriptions must be slightly altered. The proximate target in Scene 2, for example, may coincide with the distal target identified in Scene 1. The

Table 3: Scripting the Commission of Identity Theft (Time 2)

Stages	Main Tracks	Secondary Tracks
	NECESSARY SEQUENCE(S)	
Information Transfer (x^n)	Existing Accounts	Accounts by Type (e.g., Credit Card, Bank, Insurance)
	New Activities	Accounts by Type
		Employment
		Criminal Record Fraud
		Services by Type (e.g., housing, welfare)

role of guardians in authenticating the transaction(s) taking place during Time 2 is also vitally important, and any of the additional sequences mentioned (e.g., alteration, bypassing controls) might similarly be involved. In the interests of simplification, however, Table 3 suggests scripting the transfer of personal information along two main tracks (Existing Accounts and New Activities), which can then be subdivided into further tracks with regard to the specific type of activity that is committed.

Over all, progress in understanding Time 2 has been beset by a number of spatial, temporal and procedural considerations that are not easily addressed. The picture that can be assembled is thus missing many pieces – some are difficult to locate, others are literally owned by private corporations. While better surveys can be developed to tap into these areas and available victimization data can be reexamined using more refined concepts,[10] research should attempt to seek out offenders for a more in depth understanding of how different forms of identity theft can be accomplished. Particular attention should also be given to how certain activities themselves might present opportunities to continue offending or commit other forms of identity theft. As we prepare to leave this scene of the story, however, our identity thief is reaping the fruits of her labor.

Event: The Discovery of Victimization

The Bears return home to find that someone has been tampering with their belongings, and Goldilocks is ultimately discovered as the perpetrator. This moment of realization ("Someone has been sleeping in my bed!") generally captures the sense of violation experienced by all victims of identity theft, but the processes leading up to this event vary. In the identity theft version of this story, for example, Papa Bear is likely to discover his victimization through account monitoring; Baby Bear is likely to be turned down for a line of credit. The discovery of identity theft victimization can also be a process in itself, as an offender's activities are slowly uncovered over time. In other words, an ample portion of individual victims (just like the Bears) come to realize that an offender has been sleeping in their bed, eating their porridge, *and* sitting in their chairs. While some degree of harm has already been suffered at the initial point of discovery, however, victims (individuals and entities alike) now have an opportunity to mitigate their damages and deter further misuse. Closer attention should therefore be paid to the patterns of discovery, since each might set a different precedent for how victims are able to respond.

Scene 3 (Time 3): The Outcomes of Victimization

This is the point in the story where we say goodbye to Goldilocks. Sometimes the Bears eat her, sometimes she escapes; and generally speaking, this is all we know about what actually happens to identity thieves. The laws criminalizing identity theft are relatively new, and given the difficulties involved, some law enforcement agencies (the FBI, for example [Swecker, 2005]) fail to collect even basic statistics regarding the investigation or prosecution of cases, and the sentencing of offenders. A few offenders may have been "eaten" by harsher laws, but we know little about the role (if any) that different types of legislation play in either deterring offenders or bringing them to justice. These are questions that simply don't have answers yet, at least on a national scale. It would seem, however, that some identity thieves never completely learn their lesson: offending can continue long after it has been discovered, and even after the offender has been captured and imprisoned. While persistent identity theft offending may be contingent upon the type of victimization involved, particularly in relation to true-name fraud, future research should examine the reasons for why and how this can occur in greater detail.

The final scene of identity theft is also the untold part of the fairy tale, where the Bears cook some more porridge and clean up the mess in their house; maybe they call the police. Victims' actions with regard to stopping the misuse of personal information are the final defense against identity theft, however, as the best opportunities for prevention have long since passed. Patterns of victimization reporting are further related to the method of discovery; for example, victims notified of fraudulent charges on an existing account by their credit card company may not need to respond to the incident any further, although they may want to check their credit report as a precaution. The actions and procedures of secondary victims (i.e., entities) nevertheless play a vital role in the processes underlying discovery and response. The involvement of other agencies (e.g., the police, the Federal Trade Commission, credit bureaus) also warrants further analysis since even some of the least severe cases of identity theft may require victims to contact various parties (often repeatedly), who may then be expected to take action on the individual's behalf.[11]

An additional issue at this stage relates to the consequences of victimization. To briefly illustrate the differential harm caused by the two main forms of identity theft outlined above, consider the Federal Trade Commission's finding that "most victims" (63%) had no out-of-pocket expenses (Synovate, 2003:43). This figure includes: existing credit card fraud

(35.38%), existing non-credit card fraud (9.12%), and new activities (18.54%).[12] Approximately 8.28% of victims experienced more than $1,000 in out-of-pocket losses: existing credit card fraud (1.41%), existing non-credit card fraud (.94%), and new activities (5.93%). However, these figures are determined by a number of situational factors (e.g., the length of time between onset and discovery) and do not reflect the intangible costs of victimization – aside from inconvenience – that tend to accompany true-name fraud (e.g., being arrested or denied employment).

When the categories of "credit card" and "non-credit card" are combined into a single group of "existing-account fraud," however, the division between the two main forms of identity theft victimization is more pronounced. With regard to the 63% of victims who had no out-of-pocket expenses, more than half of this group (44.5%) experienced some form of existing-account misuse; the remaining 18.54% experienced some form of true-name fraud. In terms of victims who had more than $1,000 in out-of-pocket losses (8.28%), 5.93% were victims of true-name fraud and the remaining 2.35% experienced some form of existing-account misuse.[13]

The main elements for scripting this final scene are outlined in Table 4. This set of necessary sequences begins with the moment of discovery,

Table 4: Scripting the Outcomes of Identity Theft (Time 3)

Stages	Main Tracks
NECESSARY SEQUENCES	
Discovery	By Individual
	By Guardian
Individual Response (x^n)	Reports to Someone
	Doesn't Report to Anyone
Guardian Response (x^n)	Response by Type
	No Response
Individual Recovery	No Damages
	Financial Damages
	Intangible Damages by Type (e.g., arrest, denied loan)
Offending Status	Continuance
	Desistance (i.e., diversion or capture)

but not all victims of identity theft report their victimization[14] or suffer financial harm. These elements are further affected by the status of offending, as harm can sometimes result after measures have been taken to deter future misuse. Assuming the victim has contacted an agency for help, guardians' responses also become extremely important in this respect since they may either fail to act as requested or rely on an ineffective response; thus the offending behavior is implicitly allowed to continue.

The mechanisms behind this final scene of identity theft are certainly deserving of further research, but we do know more about this part of the story than any other. Scripting some actions in relation to the outcomes of identity theft may therefore be possible in an immediate sense, but eliciting more in depth information from victims is desirable. An important focus for future research should nevertheless be illuminating the links between the processes and outcomes of victimization across the entire identity theft script, as the sequences related to Time 3 are a result of the processes that occurred during the first two scenes.

CONCLUSIONS

As illustrated throughout this discussion, identity theft can be scripted in a variety ways depending upon the needs or resources of a particular project, but it can also be conceptualized as just a single scene of a much larger script (e.g., illegal immigration). Several possibilities have been offered for outlining this large expanse of identity theft territory, but these too can be summarized as the need for tracing different types of offenders, victims, guardians and targets over time.[15] While the identity theft script outlined in Figure 1 can be partially fleshed out using available data, more detailed information must be collected about the specific sequence of events involved at each stage and the interactions among various types of actors and props over time. In order to meet the challenges presented by this task, however, it is important to first survey the common ground of this phenomenon and outline a shared conceptual vocabulary for understanding its occurrence.

One of the most crucial questions about identity theft has nevertheless been the most difficult to answer: what exactly is the role of technology in identity theft, whether related to its commission, its detection or our response? The virtues of technology have been touted and its dangers minimized by those with an eye toward a cashless/paperless society; more specifically, traditional or paper-based methods for doing business have been demonized as "dangerous" in relation to the commission of identity theft (see McNally, 2008). At the same time, however, it appears that the U.S. may be in the throes of a moral panic focused on the negative consequences of modernization, specifically those resulting from technology and the Internet.[16] While the truth about technology is not this black-and-white, any response to identity theft will touch upon a delicate balance between privacy and convenience within modern societies. Technological advancements have created many opportunities for good and bad, but this issue needs to take precedence within research agendas – especially when some of the proposed technology-based methods for combating identity theft (i.e., "smart" identity cards, increased surveillance, biometric controls) may be even more intrusive than victimization itself. Prevention methods should therefore be chosen carefully and evaluated fully with regard to their intended and unintended consequences.

By necessity, the topic identity theft must be approached from a number of different angles, but this doesn't negate the fact that we're all on this journey together as both a nation and a global community. From a conceptual standpoint, the current discussion can be viewed as an invitation to stop and think for a few moments about where we are before moving forward in any direction. With a universal map, such as the one just presented, we'll at least have a better chance of determining where we've been and where we need to go from here. This expedition will not get very far, however, until we all agree that "identity theft" can only be prevented one problem at a time.

Address correspondence to: MeganM.McNally@gmail.com

Acknowledgments: In addition to Graeme Newman, I would like to thank Judith Ryder for editing and reviewing an earlier draft of this paper.

NOTES

1. There is also another level to this analogy: while fairy tales are important in a criminological sense (e.g., Mueller, 1986), there are some elements of the modern identity theft story that seem rather fantastical on their own (see McNally, 2008).

2. This observation is based on the wording of survey questions used by the Federal Trade Commission (FTC; Synovate, 2003) and the National Crime Victimization Survey (Baum, 2006). While there are differences between them, both generally ask whether a "credit card or credit card number" was misused, whether another type of "existing account" (not account number) was misused, and whether anyone had used "personal information without permission" to obtain new credit cards, loans, etc. (Baum, 2006:7; Synovate, 2003:65-66). The annual surveys conducted by Javelin Strategy & Research also use a variation of the FTC's questionnaire that doesn't appear to differ on this dimension according to the information that is available (without cost).

3. The term "synthetic fraud" has been used to describe hybrid identities composed of real and fake information, and this has been portrayed as something different from "true-name fraud" (ID Analytics, 2005a). While these semantics have caused some recent commotion (e.g., Van Dyke, 2007), the concept itself generally illustrates the importance of understanding exactly what type of personal information is obtained and how it can be misused. Although real individuals are not involved, the related issue of fabricated (or completely fake) identities also requires academic attention.

4. One useful approach for scripting identity theft would be to track different types of personal information and compare the opportunities related to the acquisition and transfer of each (e.g., a social security number vs. a driver's license number). This can only be accomplished, however, after research has unpacked the black box of "personal information."

5. The most recent study (ID Analytics, 2006) found that less than 1% of breached information had been misused, which included social security numbers. While some have interpreted this result as good news, the resiliency of social security numbers is an ongoing concern.

6. Table 1 does reflect the possibility that offenders are unsuccessful in their attempt to obtain personal information. In order to move onto Time 2 (i.e., the misuse of personal information), offenders must be successful; however, research should also examine the situations and factors that might contribute to the diversion and potential displacement of offending activities.

7. It should be kept in mind that individuals are harmed to some degree by the misappropriation of their personal information, even if it is

never misused. Aside from the common violation of privacy, there may also be physical, emotional, or financial consequences associated with the method through which it was obtained.

8. The term "assimilation" in this sense is reminiscent of the tactics used by the Borg from the futuristic series, *Star Trek*. This blended race of cyborgs (half person, half machine) plods through the universe "assimilating" everyone in their path. Captives are absorbed into the Borg collective mind through technology, which equates to having Big Brother in their heads. There is also no "I" pronoun in this society ("We are the Borg" not "I am a Borg"); thus, assimilation into the Borg represents the ultimate form of identity theft.

9. The FTC first used this classification in 2003, but Javelin Strategy & Research has recently reorganized the category of "existing account" into "card account fraud" and "non-card account fraud" (see Javelin Strategy & Research, 2007).

10. In particular, the Identity Theft Clearinghouse has collected more than one million victim complaints since its inception. While detailed information is only available to investigators, opportunities for academic analysis should be explored.

11. The potential for repeated action on the part of victims and guardians is represented in Table 4 as x^n. Other sequences may also be represented in this manner (e.g., the repeated discovery of victimization), but only the most common are presented in this table for the sake of simplicity.

12. These figures were calculated from information provided by Synovate (2003:43); the total adds to 63.04% due to rounding.

13. More consideration should also be given to understanding the distribution of costs shouldered by individual and collective victims. In particular, careful attention should be paid to how total loss figures have been estimated and how industry costs are being passed back to consumers through related services and products. For further discussion of these issues, see respectively, McNally (2008) and Newman and McNally (2005).

14. According to the Federal Trade Commission survey, 38% of victims did not contact anyone after the misuse of their personal information had been discovered (Synovate, 2003:50).

15. Also see Newman and McNally (2005) for further discussion about the procedural, temporal and spatial elements of identity theft.

16. Identity theft has been called a moral panic by Cole and Pontell (2006) in the U.S., as well as Nesbitt (2005) in the U.K. My own

dissertation research (McNally, 2008) comes to a similar, albeit not so straightforward, conclusion: the case of identity theft has many elements that are consistent with a moral panic, but the perspective itself is problematic in several respects. One possibility suggested, but not specifically examined by that research, was that identity theft is an issue on the periphery of another panic (or *phanic*) – one that centers on technology and the Internet, particularly "new" crimes such as phishing, pharming and phreaking. However, the issue of identity theft is also clearly tied into other areas often considered to be the typical objects of moral panics, including drugs, immigration, and (more recently) terrorism; thus, identity theft may be uniquely situated as a point of convergence for several different types of traditional and contemporary panics.

REFERENCES

Baum, K. (2006). *Identity theft, 2004.* Washington, DC: U.S. Department of Justice, Bureau of Justice Statistics.

Cole, S.A. and H.N. Pontell (2006). " 'Don't be a low hanging fruit': Identity theft as a moral panic," In T. Monahan (Ed.), *Surveillance and security: Technological politics and power in everyday life* (pp. 125-147). New York: Routledge.

Cornish, D. (1994). "The procedural analysis of offending and its relevance for situational prevention." In R.V. Clarke (Ed.), *Crime Prevention Studies*, vol. 3, pp. 151-196. Monsey, NY: Criminal Justice Press.

ID Analytics, Inc. (2005a, February 9). ID Analytics announces new data analysis findings; Synthetic identity fraud poses new challenges. Press release. Available at: http://www.idanalytics.com/news_and_events/2005209.html

——— (2005b, December 8). ID Analytics' first-ever national data breach analysis shows the rate of misuse of breached identities may be lower than anticipated. Press release. Available at: http://www.idanalytics.com/news_and_events/20051208.htm

——— (2006, February 9). ID Analytics analysis of 70 data breaches in 2005 shows the largest volume occurred in education sector. Press release. Available at: http://www.idanalytics.com/news_and_events/20060209.htm

Javelin Strategy & Research (2007). *2007 Identity Fraud Survey Report – consumer version: How consumers can protect themselves.* Available at: http://www.javelinstrategy.com/

McNally, M.M. (2008). *Trial by circumstance: Is identity theft a modern-day moral panic?* Unpublished Ph.D. dissertation, Rutgers University, Newark, NJ.

Mueller, G.O.W. (1986). "The criminological significance of the Grimms' fairy tales." In R.B. Bottigheimer (Ed.), *Fairy tales and society: Illusion, allusion, and paradigm* (pp. 217-227). Philadelphia, PA: University of Pennsylvania Press.

Nesbitt, F. (2005). *Identity theft exists: - but is it the real threat that those scaremongering for profit would have it?* Unpublished thesis for postgraduate M.A. in fraud management, University of Teesside, U.K.

Newman, G.R. and M.M. McNally (2005). *Identity theft literature review.*Unpublished report prepared for the U.S. National Institute of Justice. Available at: http://www.ncjrs.gov/pdffiles1/nij/grants/210459.pdf

Synovate (2003). *Federal Trade Commission – Identity Theft Survey Report.* Available at: http://www.ftc.gov/os/2003/09/synovatereport.pdf

Swecker, C. (2005). *Statement of Chris Swecker, Assistant Director, Criminal Investigative Division, Federal Bureau of Investigation, Before the Senate Judiciary Committee, April 13, 2005.* Available at: http://www.fbi.gov/congress/congress05/swecker 041305.htm

Tremblay, P. (1993). "Searching for suitable co-offenders." In R.V. Clarke and M. Felson (Eds.), *Routine Activity and Rational Choice: Advances in Criminological Theory*, pp. 17-36. New Brunswick, NJ: Transaction.

Van Dyke, J. (2007, March 21). *The hype on synthetic fraud is based on synthetic reasoning.* Available at: http://www.javelinstrategy.com/2007/03/21/the-hype-on-synthetic-fraud-is-based-on-synthetic-reasoning/

Weisburd, D., E. Waring and E.F. Chayet (2001). *White-collar crime and criminal careers.* Cambridge, UK: Cambridge University Press.

STOLEN IDENTITIES: A VICTIM SURVEY

by

Henry N. Pontell

Department of Criminology, Law and Society
University of California, Irvine

Gregory C. Brown

Department of Criminal Justice
California State University, Fullerton

Anastasia Tosouni

Department of Criminology, Law and Society
University of California, Irvine

Abstract: *This exploratory study examines patterns of identity theft offending and its impact on individual victims. Data were obtained from two victim surveys (N=378) conducted by the Identity Theft Resource Center in 2003 and 2004. Descriptive findings focus on: the location of victims and offending activities, offender characteristics, the duration and impact of victimization, child identity theft, and identity theft as a form of domestic abuse. Over all, the findings present a more detailed picture of this offense than is possible through general population surveys. Victims of identity theft suffer considerable fiscal, emotional and physical harms. This new type of victimization also differs from many traditional forms of common and white-collar crime. In order to be effective, situational crime prevention techniques* *will need to cover a much broader terrain than is usually required. While the current findings are an important first step towards this goal, the patterns observed here must be subjected to more in-depth analysis using more comprehensive data.*

INTRODUCTION

The criminological literature on crime victims focuses almost entirely on individuals who fall prey to street crime. Victimization patterns pertaining to race, gender, socioeconomic status, age, and other demographic characteristics have been documented, both in the U.S. and internationally (Catalano, 2004; Klaus, 2004; Maguire and Pastore, 2004; van Kesteren et al., 2001). Victim-offender relationships, resistance, crime characteristics and intimate violence have also been the subjects of government research (Rennison, 2003; Rennison and Rand, 2003). Victim impacts such as psychological trauma, economic and medical costs, and time and expense spent dealing with the criminal justice system have similarly been measured through the National Crime Victimization Survey (NCVS) in the United States (Maguire and Pastore, 2004). Finally, researchers have applied criminological theories in an attempt to explain victimization patterns, particularly those related to lifestyle and routine activities perspectives (Barkan, 2001:110; Miethe and Meier, 1990).

In contrast, despite well-known and serious negative consequences, there have been relatively few studies of white-collar crime victimization. This is due in no small part to the fact that such crimes are oftentimes well hidden and not immediately, if ever, known to victims. White-collar and corporate offenses may also involve diffuse victimization that affects entire segments of a population, rather than identifiable individual victims who will report such occurrences (Rosoff et al., 2007; Shichor et al., 2001; Titus et al., 1995). It has also been noted that victim embarrassment as well as a lack of compensation for crime losses results in a significant under-reporting of such crimes (Shichor et al., 2001:86). Nonetheless, one notable study conducted by Neal Shover and his colleagues (1994:96) found that "some victims of white-collar crime endure enormous long-term pain and suffering," in a manner similar to victims of street crime. Moreover, elements inherent in fraud victimization may reinforce public and victim perceptions that they acted foolishly, and are therefore more blameworthy with regard to their own victimization. Victims of investment scams, for example, can be easily viewed as "greedy" or "non-vigilant," and not as "ideal victims" who put adequate effort into self-protection (Shichor et al., 2001:83).

Another reason for limited concern about such victims has to do with the relatively lenient nature of official reactions to white-collar offenses and their perpetrators. As noted by Shichor and his colleagues: "Generally investment fraud victims are seen as economically well-to-do people; therefore they do not seem to need as much sympathy because they can take their losses with relative ease. The professional interest in these victims is limited also among victimologists, a fact that can be seen in the contents of victimology textbooks" (ibid:84). The neglect of fraud victims, it has been reasonably argued, stems from what can be considered a "paternalistic" approach by some social scientists in an attempt to be supportive of poor, vulnerable or disenfranchised victims of common crime. This, coupled with the use of such victims by more conservative interest groups to justify stricter laws and policies against street crime, has resulted in victim compensation and assistance programs that target the needs of street crime victims. Measures such as a "Victim's Bill of Rights," which has been passed in numerous states in the U.S., not only have focused on concern for victims, but arguably have been thinly veiled attempts to increase punishment and limit the rights of common criminals (ibid). Supported by business groups, as well as women's organizations and other social activists, these have efforts focused attention on crimes against women, sex crimes, domestic violence and other social ills, while at the same time diverting attention and interest from victims of fraud and other white-collar offenses (ibid:85).

There are many reasons to believe that fraud victims suffer just as many, if not more negative experiences, than victims of common crime. The collapse of Lincoln Savings and Loan during the savings and loan crisis in the U.S. during the 1980s, for example, involved numerous retirees who were duped into investing their life savings in what were soon to become worthless junk bonds issued by Charles Keating's American Continental Corporation. One report noted that an elderly investor became so distraught after losing his $200,000 nest egg that he killed himself (Connelly, 1990). Long-term effects of fraud victimization, such as sleep disorders over fear of additional financial losses, have also been reported in past research (Shichor et al., 1996). Moreover, since fraud involves deceit, victims may be more likely to engage in "self-blaming" than victims of many common crimes. That is, being deceived into participating in your own victimization can carry psychological costs that outweigh the degree of financial harm associated with the crime (Levi, 1992).

The Emergence of Identity Theft

Over the past decade, a new major offense has emerged that shares many characteristics with other financial and economic crimes: identity theft (IDT). Financial frauds have been part of the economic crime landscape for many years. Since the classic writings of Donald Cressey (1953) on embezzlement and Edwin Lemert (1958) on check forgers, new financial frauds have emerged on the economic scene. Various bank frauds, computer-assisted thefts, credit card frauds, securities offenses, and a host of other economic crimes have become a significant part of everyday business transactions (Rosoff et al., 2007). The proliferation of new technology and the rise of the Internet have fostered new crime forms, such as auction fraud and online banking fraud, which have already begun to wreak economic havoc on consumers and the emerging e-commerce system. The increasing use and accessibility of electronic means for personal banking, for example, have created new opportunities for fraud that have already resulted in significant victimization. One recent major survey found that during the past few years more than 4 million consumers had been victimized by checking account takeovers – when a thief added his information to an existing account, changed the mailing address or made other alterations in order to obtain unlimited access to it – with half that number saying the thefts had occurred within the past 12 months, indicating a sharp increase in the activity (Sullivan, 2004). Many of these scams were simple low-tech frauds, committed by organized crime rings and individual criminals. The cumulative effects even for these, however, can be quite large. In addition to the significant amount of financial losses, there is the resulting personal trauma for victims who can spend months or years reestablishing their economic identities (ibid).

Identity theft as a crime category includes both old and new offenses. It is related to and facilitates new crimes made possible by technological advances (most notably the networked computer) and new financial and organizational arrangements that include large amounts of identity information stored in numerous public and private databases (e.g., on-line banking, credit information, and e-business records). These new technologies and means to conduct financial transactions have increased the value of "identities," so that claiming to be another individual, based on information corroborated in various databases, will result in a financial institution extending credit and/or releasing funds to the claimant. The same new technologies and financial arrangements have facilitated the theft of highly valued identities through practices such as "hacking" into large databases. The new economic order, much of which is based upon electronic transactions and similarly stored identity data, has produced a "crime facilitative environment" (Needleman and Needleman, 1979) in which new forms of lawbreaking flourish.

On the other hand, identity theft characteristically involves older forms of crime and financial fraud. In what has been called the "identity theft panic" (Cole and Pontell, 2006), the term "identity theft" has been used to denote a wide variety of offenses such as checking frauds, financial crimes, counterfeiting, forgery, auto theft using false documentation, trafficking in human beings, and terrorism – all of which existed as crime categories before the diffusion of the term "identity theft." Widespread media publicity regarding the dire and dramatic impact on victims has been one of the major reasons for the creation of the new offense of identity theft. In reviewing the current literature, Graeme Newman and Megan McNally (2005:12) note the importance of victimization issues in the creation of the crime of identity theft in U.S. federal law:

> It is clear that these identity theft-related crimes are not new crimes at all, but rather are old crimes enhanced by the use of, or theft of, stolen identities. However it is our assessment that the federal law derives not so much from those old crimes, but from the wide publicity in the late 1990s of victims of identity theft. These were victims who were repeatedly victimized over a period of time from months to sometimes years and who were unable to get back their identities or were unable to convince credit issuing and reporting authorities of their loss. The publicity gave rise to a series of Congressional hearings, which eventually resulted in the Identity Theft Act of 1998.

In order to better understand identity theft and its impacts, the Identity Theft Resource Center (ITRC), based in San Diego, California, collects systematic data on identity theft victimization. The award-winning non-profit program is dedicated exclusively to identity theft victims. ITRC was founded by a victim of identity theft and its stated goals are to support victim self-advocacy; broaden consumer, corporate, governmental and legislative awareness and understanding of identity theft issues; and decrease the potential victim population by increasing access to information through various service projects. In order to better understand the patterns of identity theft and its impact on victims, the current study presents an analysis of data from two victimization surveys conducted by the ITRC in 2003 and 2004.

THE ITRC SURVEYS: METHODOLOGICAL ISSUES

Between October and mid-December 2004, surveys were e-mailed to 1,344 identity theft victims who had contacted the ITRC between August 2003 and October 2004[1] either by e-mail or telephone, and for whom there was a valid return e-mail address. Two percent of those contacted said that they could not complete the survey due to the emotional impact of their victimization. There were 199 e-mails returned as non-deliverable, representing 14.8% of the original sample. A total of 197 persons completed the online survey, producing a response rate of 14.7%. Those not responding for any number of other reasons totaled 914, or 68%. Detailed information was not available for the 2003 survey, which was administered approximately one year earlier.

The survey did not ask for any demographic information from respondents, making it difficult to assess whether the sample is representative of the victim population. The responses to certain questions, however, can be compared to those obtained in other studies to see whether there is any correspondence with national patterns; and as will be shown below, this clearly appears to be the case. Moreover, ITRC staff had established through their conversations with those in the original sample that they were all indeed *confirmed identity theft victims.*[2]

The surveys were designed to obtain information regarding the experiences of identity theft victims, and cover a broad array of areas. Given the relative paucity of information regarding the experiences of victims, the goal was to create a baseline from which trends and patterns could be discerned in future studies. Another major strength of the survey is that it focuses solely on victims and their cases, providing specific information regarding the crimes involved as well as the effects of victimization. Recent reports and studies cite the difficulties that complicate the measurement of identity theft, as well as patterns of reporting to law enforcement agencies, banks and credit card companies, and government and private organizations (see, for example, Newman and McNally, 2005). Ultimately, such information is useful for educational outreach, policy making and law enforcement purposes, and for the education of IDT victims, and the public. Learning more about ID theft victimization and the experiences of victims can also provide data useful for allocating resources toward more effective responses by the criminal justice system, private industry, government agencies and victim assistance organizations generally, and for crime prevention strategies more specifically.

It must also be noted that several issues seriously complicate the measurement of identity theft (National Institute of Justice, 2005). First, a victim is unable to report the crime until it has been discovered, which may not be for some time. Second, a crime is not always reported when it is discovered, and, if it is, it may be reported to any number of organizations and government agencies, making it difficult if not impossible to include the actual number of reported episodes from these disparate sources. Third, many law enforcement agencies do not record such crimes in a uniform manner because categorizations for such acts are evolving and may remain unclear to the personnel responsible for this task. Fourth, the FBI's Uniform Crime Reports have not, until very recently, had an offense category of "identity theft," so that trends in such offenses could not be studied over time. Fifth, given the nature of the phenomenon of identity theft, personal identifying information can be stolen *en masse* through computers and the Internet without it being discovered or reported for long periods of time, if it is ever known or reported at all. (For example, in the case of deceased-person frauds where there is no living victim to report the crime, family members may never discover it.) And finally, the current capacity of the enforcement system to collect information on identity theft is limited by the multi-jurisdictional possibilities inherent in the crime itself, in that a victim may reside in one state, the offender in another, and the victimized business or financial institution in yet another.

A survey conducted by Synovate (2003) and the initial findings of the 2004 U.S. National Crime Victimization Survey (NCVS; Baum, 2006) are also relevant to the patterns of victimization reported here. Since the surveys conducted by the ITRC did not include demographic information, it is impossible to compare patterns related to the personal characteristics of victims. For example, the 2003 Synovate survey found that Hispanics and African Americans were twice as likely as Asians or Whites to experience the most serious type of fraud, and that middle-aged persons tended to become the victims of larger dollar amount frauds. This survey polled 4,057 consumers and found that 4.6% had discovered in the past year that they had been victimized by identity theft. About half of the victims knew how their identities had been stolen, and victims' family members were reported as the most common perpetrators.[3]

The initial findings of the NCVS (Baum, 2006) suggest that identity theft is more concentrated in affluent households.[4] The Synovate survey further suggests that victims play a major role in discovering identity theft:

over half of the victims reported the theft after their purse or wallet had been stolen, or after noticing aberrations on their paper or electronic financial account statements. The stolen information was typically used for about six months, with victims of lower income and educational levels having their information used for longer periods of time. After discovery, it usually took three months to resolve the victim's financial status. About a third of victims of new account fraud knew their imposter, and half of them reported this person as a family member.

A number of issues regarding victimization still remain to be investigated, including: the nature of resulting personal and family harms, the amount of time and money lost in resurrecting one's identity, the direct financial costs to victims and businesses, the victimization of children, and other consequences such as the false arrest of victims for crimes committed by their imposters. Experts have also noted that victim experiences in obtaining assistance from the police, financial institutions, credit card companies, businesses and government agencies, as well as the varieties of identity theft, are not yet well understood. Moreover, and perhaps most importantly, from a policy perspective it is important to identify the proportion of persons who suffer significantly from identity theft, and precisely how they are affected, as opposed to those who experience only a minor inconvenience. The ITRC survey included 46 questions regarding the victim, the type of crime committed, and the effects of victimization.[5] The exploratory analysis that follows is therefore intended to shed light on both the nature of identity theft and its effects on victims.

FINDINGS[6]

Victim Location

Almost 19% of the sample resided in California (38 persons), followed by Florida (9%), Texas (6%), and New York (5%). In 2004, these states ranked in the top seven for the number of identity theft complaints received by the Federal Trade Commission (2005).[7] About half (49%) of the respondents noted that their identity information had been used in their home state, about a third (32%) said that it had been used in another state, and another 19% said it had been used in both.

Type of ID Theft

Respondents were asked what types of ID theft they experienced. The vast majority reported being victimized by financial ID theft only (66%):

9% were victimized by financial in combination with criminal ID theft, about 8% in combination with "cloning," (where a criminal acquires personal identifiers and then impersonates someone else in order to conceal his or her true identity from authorities), and about 6% by a combination of all three (financial, criminal, and cloning). Two-thirds of the 2004 sample (66%) reported that their personal information had been used to open a new credit account in their name, followed by purchasing cellular telephone service (28%), making charges to the victim's existing credit card (27%), making charges over the Internet (22%), purchasing and making charges to new telephone service (19%), and purchasing a new cable television or energy utility account (18%).[8] Compared to the 2003 survey data, there were no significant differences other than a doubling in the proportion of those reporting that their information was used to purchase cable or utility accounts (from 9% in 2003 to 18% in 2004).[9] Non-financial forms of identity theft were also reported: 12% said that thieves had committed financial crimes that resulted in warrants being issued in their name, followed by 10% who said that a counterfeit driver's license was produced with their information, and 8% who reported that a real driver's license had been obtained.

Estimate of Business Loss

Respondents estimated the total dollar value to the business community of all charges placed on fraudulent accounts in their name. About three-quarters of respondents in both years responded to this question. When statistical outliers are removed from the sample, there was about a 20% increase in the average estimated business loss reported by respondents in 2004 as compared to 2003 ($49,254 and $41,717, respectively). Victims were also asked if they knew the total number of credit cards that had been granted fraudulently using their personal information. Almost half the sample (46%) responded none,[10] while over a quarter of respondents noted that one to three cards had been issued. Another 22% reported four to ten new cards, and the percentages drop off dramatically past this point.

Characteristics of the ID Thief

Survey respondents also provided information to a series of questions regarding their imposter. Table 1 shows that over 90% of victims in the 2004 survey were aware of the status of the person who used their information, as compared to 86% of the victims from the year before.

Table 1: Current Status of Imposter

	YEAR	
STATUS	2004 Percent (N)	2003 Percent (N)
Active	26.4	42.5
Not active	50.8	42.6
Arrested	4.1	N/A[a]
Convicted	9.6	N/A[a]
Missing/Don't know	9.1	13.8
TOTAL	100.0 (197)	100.0 (181)

a. Category not included in 2003 survey.

About half (51%) of the 2004 survey respondents believed that the offender was not presently active in using their information. About a quarter (26%) noted that the offender was still active, which is significantly lower than what was reported by 2003 respondents (43%). About 14% reported that they knew the offender had been arrested and/or convicted.

About half of the 2004 sample (54%) checked a category other than "unknown" when asked if they knew the identity of their imposter, indicating that they had information about the status of their imposter. This is somewhat higher than those who reported knowing the status of their imposter in 2003 (41%). The percentages in Table 2 are based on those who did not respond to this question by saying the identity thief was "unknown."[11] A little over a third who did not answer "unknown" in 2004 stated that the person was a relative, as compared to only a quarter of respondents in 2003. Almost a quarter of those in 2004 responded that the person was an ex-spouse or a significant other, as compared to only 10% in 2003. In 2004, 14% said that it was an employee of a business who had their information, as compared to about a quarter of respondents in 2003. Between 12% and 20% said it was a friend or a roommate.

In a separate question, respondents in the 2004 survey were asked to check off the characteristics of their imposters about which they were certain. Multiple answers could be chosen by respondents. Whereas 87 people were not certain about the offender's characteristics, 113 (57%) checked at least one of the options (Table 3). Of these respondents, 47% responded that the imposter had committed other types of crimes as well.

Table 2: Imposter Relationship to Victim

	YEAR	
IMPOSTER IS:	2004 Percent[a] (N)	2003 Percent[a] (N)
Relative	38.3	23.9
Ex-spouse or significant other	23.4	9.9
Employee of business with their information	14.0	26.8
Friend/Roommate	12.1	19.7
Co-worker	5.6	8.5
Neighbor	2.8	1.4
Caregiver of elder/disable	0.0	2.8
Missing[b]	11.2 (12)	18.3 (13)

a. Based on 107 respondents (54.3%) in 2004 and 71 (39.2%) in 2003 who did not check "unknown" as their answer.
b. Refers to people who did not check ANY of the available options (including "unknown").

About 34% said that the offender had a history of needing money to support an addiction caused by narcotics or alcohol use, or a shopping or gambling problem. A total of 31% said it was simply about money and that it didn't matter how the person got it, and an additional 28% responded that the person had done this to other family members as well. Other imposter characteristics were listed by 22% of the respondents, including the offender being a repeat ID thief (3%), an illegal alien (2.5%), or mentally ill (2.5%).

How Victims Found Out About Their Identity Thefts

Of those responding to this question, 12% said that they first found out about their victimization after they were contacted by a collection agency regarding unpaid bills. This was followed in frequency by 10% who said they were contacted by a creditor demanding payment on late bills, and 10% who were contacted by a credit company after unusual activity was seen on their account, such as a suspicious credit application or large purchases. Another 9% reported that they first found out after they were denied credit or a loan, and 14% found out through noticing unauthorized charges on their credit card bill or that funds were missing from their

Table 3: Imposter Characteristics as Reported by Victims (2004, N=113)

IMPOSTER:	N	Percent[a]
Has committed other types of crime	53	46.9
Has a history of needing money due to narcotics, alcohol, shopping or gambling	39	34.5
Steals because wants money, regardless of the means	35	31.0
Has done this to other family members (Family IDT)	32	28.3
Is part of an organized crime unit	11	9.7
Steals because it is fun	11	9.7
Has a history of other crimes, so gives victim's name instead	10	8.8
Is just doing it to prove that he/she can	9	8.0
Is doing this to hide – i.e., to avoid child support/arrest	8	7.1
Did this due to a single act of desperation	6	5.3
Other	25	22.1
Total	113	100.0

a. Percentages are based on the 113 people (56.4%) in the sample who answered this question.

bank account. Over half of the sample (55%) discovered their victimization through these six means; another 9% reported means not included in the categories present on the survey.

Victimization Time Periods

Respondents were asked a series of questions about the time periods of their victimization (Tables 4 and 5). The first question asked the number of months between the first recorded incident of identity theft and the discovery that their identity had been stolen. Over a third (37.5%) of those surveyed in 2004 reported that they had found out within three months, as compared to almost half of the respondents in the 2003 survey (48%). Between 11% and 14% had found out between in either four to six months or seven to twelve months in both survey groups. Of those responding in 2004, 18% said that it took them four years or more to discover that their identities had been misused, as compared to only 9% in the 2003 sample.

Table 4: Time Between First Incident and Discovery by Victims

	YEAR	
MONTHS PASSED	**2004** Percent (N=192)	**2003** Percent (N=174)
0-3	37.5	47.7
4-6	10.9	12.0
7-12	13.5	12.6
13-18	4.2	8.7
19-23	7.8	4.6
2-3 years	8.3	5.2
4 years and more	17.7	9.2
Total	100.0	100.0
Missing	2.5 (5)	4.0 (7)

Table 5: Time of Involvement for Victims Who Considered Their Case Closed

	YEAR	
MONTHS PASSED	**2004** Percent[a] (N=56)	**2003** Percent[a] (N=65)
0-3	16.1	10.8
4-6	32.1	26.2
7-12	14.3	23.1
13-18	16.1	16.9
19-23	5.4	9.2
2-3 years	5.4	6.2
4 years	3.6	6.2
More than 4 years	7.2	1.5
Total	100.0	100.0

a. Based on the 56 people (28.4%) in 2004 and 65 people (35.9%) in 2003 who answered this question and who did not also answer that their case was open.

Almost half (48%) of the 2004 respondents and more than a half (57%) of the 2003 survey respondents stated that they considered their case closed (e.g., an arrest had been made, or there had been no new ID theft activity for a prolonged period).[12] In both years, 26% to 32% responded that they had been dealing with their case for a period of four to six months, whereas for about 11% to 16% of respondents, their involvement did not exceed three months. A considerably higher number of respondents reported spending more than four years on their cases in 2004 compared to those who responded in 2003 (7% and 2%, respectively). Approximately 16% to 17% of respondents reported having spent between 13 and 18 months on the case; however, a higher number of respondents in 2003 (23%) as compared to those in 2004 (11%) responded that they had been dealing with their case for a period of seven months to one year.

Of those surveyed in 2003 and 2004, 42% and 48% (respectively) responded that they still considered their case to be open in that no one was arrested, and that their information might still be available for criminal use (Table 6).[13] A higher percentage of 2004 as compared to 2003 respon-

Table 6: Time of Involvement for Victims Whose Case Is Considered Unresolved

	YEAR	
NUMBER OF MONTHS	2004 Percent[a] (N=94)	2003 Percent[a] (N=76)
0-3	6.4	5.3
4-6	27.7	17.1
7-12	13.8	6.6
13-18	13.8	10.5
19-23	2.1	15.8
2-3 years	12.8	7.9
4-5 years	12.8	13.2
6-7 years	5.3	11.8
8-10 years	3.2	3.9
10	2.1	7.2
Total	100.0 (94)	100.0 (76)

a. Based on the 94 people (47.7%) in 2004 and the 76 people (42%) in 2003 who answered this question and who did not also answer that their case was closed.

dents reported involvement between four months to a year (42% versus 24%, respectively). Moreover, fewer respondents in 2004 (11%), compared to those in 2003 (23%), said that their case has been keeping them involved for six years or more. Over all, of those responding that their case was still open in that the imposter(s) had not been arrested and may still be using their personal information, 37% stated that they had been working on their case for two years or more in 2004 as compared to 44% in 2003. These percentages are significantly higher than for those who reported their cases closed (16% in 2004 and 14% in 2003).

Another question asked how long the identity theft had affected the victim's life, regardless of whether the case was closed or still open. The intent here was to measure non-emotional impacts, such as the ability to obtain credit, clear accounts, obtain or hold a job, and any effects on insurance or credit rates. A portion of the sample (15%) responded that their lives were not affected at all, and another 7% did not answer the question. Of the 78% of persons who did respond, the most frequent answers were four to five years (16%), one to six months (13%), and 13-18 months (11%). Over all, 22% reported that the theft had affected their lives for one month to one year, 23% reported effects of one to three years, and 32% reported effects of four years or more.[14]

Effects of Victimization on Financial Status

Respondents who reported that the ID theft case was still affecting their lives were asked to specify how by selecting from a list of items (Table 7). They were instructed to check all that applied to their situation: 68% of the sample responded to this question, and almost half of these (48%) checked more than one category of effect. Almost half of the respondents in the sample (46%) answered that loan and credit acquisitions had been negatively affected by their case of ID theft. In addition, 40% of respondents noted that they had been denied credit, and 29% replied that collection agencies had called them. When asked whether they knew if their imposter had continued to use their information after they were arrested, 6% of the 2004 survey respondents said that they had, as compared to 11% in 2003. Other respondents replied that they hadn't been used, that they didn't know, or they didn't answer the question at all.

Respondents were also asked whether they had been able to eliminate all of the negative items from their credit reports and/or criminal records. The vast majority of those who answered this question in both samples

Table 7: Manner in Which Victim's Financial Life Was Affected (2004, N=197)

EFFECT	N	Percent[a]
Credit or loan acquisition affected	91	46.2
Credit denied	79	40.1
Collection agencies calling	57	28.9
Credit card rates increased	38	19.3
Insurance rates increased	32	16.2
Tenancy acquisition affected	28	14.2
Credit card cancelled	22	11.2
Employment acquisition affected	21	10.7
Criminal record un-cleared	14	7.1

a. Total exceeds 100% because respondents were able to check off more than one effect.

(70% in 2004 and 66% in 2003) responded that there was still negative information on their records. Reasons for not being able to clear their records were also ascertained, and respondents were instructed to check all answers that applied to their situation. Of the 64% in the sample who reported at least one reason, almost half (about 48%) checked more than one. Credit agencies, either by putting negative information back in records (27%) or by not removing it in the first place (25%), topped the list of reasons for victims' inability to clear their records. Following these reasons were: victims saying that their fraud alerts were ignored (19%), victims giving up due to lack of time (18%), and having records re-sold to new agencies who then hounded the victims for charges incurred by the identity thieves (15%).

Child ID Theft

A series of questions were also asked about the victimization of children by ID theft; 33 respondents (17%) reported the theft of a child's identity. The median age of these victims when the crime began was 11 years old, which was close to the reported mean age of 10. Both the median and mean age was 18 when the theft was discovered. The median age of the victims was 19 years, and the mean age was a little more than 20. Of the 11 valid responses regarding the identity of the imposter for victims still under the age of 18, 45% were mothers and about a third were fathers.

Thus, for current child victims, in over three-quarters of the cases the imposters were their parents. A similar pattern existed for victims now over 18, with more than 60% of imposters being reported as parents. About a quarter of imposters were reported as strangers. These results must be interpreted cautiously, however, because of the small numbers upon which they are based. As shown in Table 8, a police report had been filed in almost half (46%) of the cases where the child ID victim was over 18. Almost a third of the respondents wanted to settle the matter without the police, and 23% reported doing nothing yet. Another 15% reported that they had been successful in having creditors obtaining the money owed from the imposter, and then having had their own reports cleared.

ID Theft as Continued Abuse to Domestic Victims

If the ID thief had also committed domestic harassment and/or abuse against the victim, respondents were asked whether they felt that the identity theft was being used as a way of continuing to harass or abuse them (Table 9). Of the 31 persons (16%) who answered this question, more than half answered in the affirmative. In other words, 16% of ID theft victims in the sample were also victims of domestic harassment and/or abuse by the imposter, and slightly more than half felt that the ID theft was being used as a way to continue this abuse and/or harassment.

Deceased-Person Fraud

Another question asked whether the victim was dead at the time of the ID theft ("deceased-person fraud"). While two persons reported that this

Table 8: Measures Taken to Resolve the Situation of Child Victims Currently Over 18 (2004)

REMEDY	N	Percent[a]
Police report	6	46.2
Want to settle without police	4	30.8
Nothing yet	3	23.1
Cleared report	2	15.4
Family will pay	0	0.0
Other	4	30.8

a. Based on the 13 people (6.6%) in the sample who answered the previous question. Some answered more than one category of response.

Table 9: Offenders Using IDT as a Form of Domestic Abuse (2004)

IDT AS FORM OF DOMESTIC ABUSE	N	Percent[a]
No	15	48.4
Yes	16	51.6
Total	31	100.0
N/A	166	84.3

a. Based on 31 people (15.7%) in the sample who reported domestic abuse.

was the case in 2003, none reported that this was the case in 2004. Deceased person fraud by many accounts occurs regularly, however it is not likely to be tapped by a victimization survey for a variety of reasons. In particular, the victim's family is not likely to know about it; and if they do become aware of the theft, there is little need for them to do anything if it does not directly affect their lives. The victims in such cases are most likely government entitlement programs such as Social Security, Medicare, and other public and private benefit programs. These organizations would need to conduct separate studies in order to determine the extent of this problem.

Where the Information Was Obtained

The 2004 data show that about two-thirds of respondents reported knowing the source of stolen information.[15] Of these, 39% stated that a friend or family member was the source of the stolen information. This was followed by 11% who said that it was taken from their mail, and 26% who responded that it was from a source not listed in the survey.

Experiences with Organizations After Victimization

Respondents were also asked a series of questions about their experiences with organizations after their victimization in order to determine the types and levels of services provided to them. For each question they were asked to check all of the categories that applied to their particular situation. These responses are potentially useful for targeting areas of consumer services for ID theft victims that are in need of improvement.

About half of the 2003 and 2004 respondents said that most credit issuers required a police report. About half of each survey group replied that it had taken more than three phone calls to resolve the problem with the credit issuer. In contrast, only 10% to 13% said that they had resolved the problem in less than three calls. About one-third of each group noted that it had taken more than three letters to solve the problem, while only 6% in the 2004 sample and 13% in the 2003 survey said it had taken three or fewer letters. Whether these patterns reflect a lack of diligence on the part of the organization or the victim, or some combination of both, does not really matter in terms of the reported negative victim impacts.

Over 40% of the respondents in both surveys stated that at least one company had refused to clear their account even after they had provided evidence of the theft. More than 30% in both surveys responded that credit issuers had turned their account over to a collection agency *after* the company had "cleared" them from responsibility for the charges.[16] Fewer than a quarter of those surveyed in both groups reported that it was easy to find a phone number to reach the credit-issuing companies. Not surprisingly, less than 17% of each sample stated that they were pleased with the level of service provided.

Victim experiences with the credit reporting companies Experian, Equifax, and TransUnion were also obtained. In all three cases, fewer than half of the survey respondents reported that information was easily understood in the format provided. Only about one-half of respondents reported receiving their credit reports within two weeks time, with the highest percentage being reported for Experian (57%). Only about one-fifth of respondents said that it was easy to speak with someone from the company after receiving their report, and similar numbers reported that the person was helpful and answered most, if not all of their questions. About 40% of respondents said that they had sent a dispute letter to the credit bureau, but less than one-fifth reported that the company had removed misinformation and errors from their report after their first request to do so. About a third of the victims reported that they had to send dispute information to the credit reporting companies repeatedly.

About two-thirds of the 2004 survey respondents said that they had contacted the police regarding their victimization, compared to over three-quarters of the 2003 group. Reported patterns of police-victim interaction show that police took a report during the first contact in over half of the cases. In about one-quarter of the cases, victims reported having had to contact the police more than once to have a report taken; 15% to 21% reported that a report was never taken. Fewer than half of the victims responded that they had received a written report, or that there was a detective assigned to their case. Less than 10% reported that they were kept informed at least monthly. Between 40% and 59% reported that they had contacted more than one police department, and about half of the respondents felt bounced from one agency to another with no one willing to help.

Impacts on Victims: Financial and Personal

Victims were asked a series of questions to measure the impacts of ID theft in both financial and personal terms. These were grouped broadly under financial impacts, the effects of the case on their personal relationships and family, the impacts when the offender was a family member, and the effects on their general emotional state and mental health. The reported financial impacts of identity theft on victims are reported in Table 10. Given that the ranges vary greatly between the two survey groups on most items (even after outliers were removed), both the median and mean were used to measure the degree of central tendency (average) for these variables. Results are reported with and without outliers where applicable.

The minimum mean hours spent actively trying to fix things in both groups when outliers were removed varied between 265 and 436, with half of the respondents spending 100 hours or less. Based on their salaries, if victims were paid for this time, they would have earned (on average) between $14,340 in 2003 and $1,820 in 2004. The medians were $3,350 and $4,000 in 2003 and 2004, respectively. The survey groups reported missing on average between 72 and 90 hours of work time due to their victimization (after outliers were removed), and an average of between 53 and 65 hours of lost vacation or personal leave time. Respondents also noted average expenses of between $851 and $1,378 for such items as phone calls, affidavits, travel, and notaries, among other costs. The reported average medical expenses incurred to restore their physical or emotional health were $810 in the 2003 sample, and $614 in the 2004 group (after outliers were removed). The average hours spent on these medical services was 46 in both surveys (after outliers were removed).

When asked how the ID theft case had affected important relationships in their lives, 43% of both samples responded that it had created a stressed family life, perhaps due to their displaced anger and frustration. In the 2004 survey, 40% stated that their families were supportive, while about a quarter of respondents in both groups said that their family didn't

Table 10: Financial Impact on Victims

	Mean (w/o outlier)	Median	SD (w/o outlier)	Range (w/o outlier)
Hours Spent[a]				
YEAR				
2004 (N=158)	331 (264.7)	100	708 (402.6)	3-5840 (2000)
2003 (N=143)	773 (435.6)	100	3481 (1112)	2-38705 (9000)
Earnings Lost (USD)				
YEAR				
2004 (N=150)	1820	4000	68210	0-650000
2003 (N=138)	14340	3350	32240	100-220000
Work Hours[a]				
YEAR				
2004 (N=132)	109 (90)	10	340 (264)	0-2560 (1600)
2003 (N=112)	275 (72)	20	1535 (230)	0-12800 (2080)
Vacation Hours				
YEAR				
2004 (N=119)	64.5	16	167	0-1000
2003 (N=98)	52.5	16	128	0-1000
Expenses (USD)				
YEAR				
2004 (N=149)	851	100	3109	0-25000
2003 (N=123)	1378	150	3853	0-30000
Medical Expenses[a]				
YEAR				
2004 (N=96)	1153 (614)	0	3974 (1327)	0-30000 (6000)
2003 (N=68)	2403.5 (810)	37.5	94 (1732)	0-60000 (10000)
Medical Hours[a]				
YEAR				
2004 (N=92)	46.2	0	151.5	0-1000
2003 (N=68)	192.5 (46)	1	1214 (132)	0-10000 (840)

a. Excluded outliers include the following cases: cases 1 (5,840) and 9 (5,040) in the 2004 data, and cases 3 (10,400) and 27 (38,705) in the 2003 data for *Hours Spent;* case 9 (2,560) in the 2004 data, and cases 3 (10,000) and 34 (12,800) in the 2003 data for *Work Hours*; cases 15 (23,000) and 37 (30,000) in 2004, and cases 162 (75,000) and 81 (60,000) in 2003 for *Medical Expenses*; and case 146 (10,000) in 2003 for *Medical Hours*.

understand why they were feeling as they did. A quarter of both samples responded that it had affected their children who were aware of the situation, and about the same number replied that they felt betrayed by those close to them who didn't want to understand their feelings. Fewer than 17% in both groups responded that their "significant other took over many of the tasks to clear up this mess." Finally, 9% and 16% in the 2004 and 2003 surveys, respectively, responded that their marital relationship was "on the rocks" or ended as a result of their victimization.

A series of questions were asked regarding the impact of victimization when the imposter was a family member. About one-third of the 2004 survey group answered these questions, as compared to only one-fifth of those in the 2003 group. In total, 43% of those responding in the 2004 sample, as compared to a little over half of those who responded in 2003, said that the imposter had a history of needing money due to narcotics, gambling, alcohol or shopping. In the 2004 survey, about half responded that the person had committed other crimes, as compared to over three-quarters in 2003. Victims also reported that the imposter had done this to other family members as well (51% in 2004 and 38% in 2003). While a significant number of respondents said they felt torn about what to do (36% in 2004 and 24% in 2003), fewer of them responded that they didn't feel right about reporting the theft to police (27% and 14%). The families of victims were not likely to tell the victim to drop the case (13% and 14%), and two-thirds of the 2004 respondents reported that their families supported them in trying to force the thief to take responsibility for his or her actions, or report the crime to police. Victims generally did not report that their families were ashamed or remained in denial (31% and 22%), or that their families would turn against them if they took action against the person (19% and 14%). Thirty-nine percent of 2004 respondents and over half of 2003 respondents reported that the imposter used identity theft to destroy their reputation.

Finally, victims were asked to report on their emotional state as a result of the crime. Two questions were asked that were intended to measure general feelings, as compared to longer lasting symptoms of two months or more or that caused them concern because of their severity. The most frequent categories chosen were anger, feeling betrayed, feeling unprotected by police or by laws, deep fears regarding personal financial security, having a sense of powerlessness or helplessness, and having sleep disturbances.

CONCLUSION

The findings reveal a number of patterns that are worthy of further analysis. While general population surveys are useful in describing general demographic patterns and longitudinal trends, a survey of victims allows greater detail regarding the crimes, the characteristics of perpetrators, and the impacts of the offenses. The data from the ITRC surveys show that identity theft victims suffer considerable fiscal and physical harms. Their victimization also differs from many traditional forms of common and white-collar crime in that IDT is more likely to be repetitive over time, the victim may or may not be aware of it while it is happening, and it continues to have harmful impacts during the period in which victims reestablish their financial identities.

The findings are also useful for suggesting crime prevention strategies regarding identity theft, although specific actions that need to be taken will vary widely given the myriad ways in which a person's identity can be stolen and used in subsequent criminal activities. For example, a significant proportion of respondents reported knowing who the imposter was, which indicates the need to be protective of personal information even around those whom one knows well. But individual responsibility only goes so far. A significant number of respondents also did not know who their imposter was, nor did they know how their identity information had been stolen. They may or may not have been vigilant with their personal data: the manner in which the information it was stolen could have more to do with systemic and organizational breakdowns or leaks rather than with individual irresponsibility. The significant presence of identity theft committed by family members, especially as it involves children, points to the need for better authentication systems and monitoring by financial institutions and government agencies so that parents are not able to use their children's names for fiscal gain, which subsequently leaves their financial identities in shambles when they finally come of age. More extensive public education campaigns may be useful to a point in creating individual awareness regarding the importance of securing personal data and responsible computer use. But at the same time, there is also a need for better regulatory policy aimed at protecting information in public and proprietary databases that are not within the purview of individual control.

Some important caveats are necessary despite the significance of these findings for informing both research and crime prevention policies regarding identity theft. First, and foremost, these data are from a self-selected group of victims who contacted the ITRC, and who subsequently agreed to respond to a survey. Moreover, the lack of questions regarding important demographic variables makes it impossible to ascertain whether or not these victims are truly representative of identity theft victims found in general population surveys.

Other problems also remain in ascertaining the true nature of identity theft and corresponding crime prevention strategies. One major problem is that large amounts of identity information are stolen from databases maintained by educational institutions, banks, credit reporting agencies, or related businesses that may not come to the attention of victims for some time (Colker and Menn, 2005; Connell, 2004). In the first 8 months of 2005 alone, at least 96 security breaches occurred in the U.S., affecting the identity information of nearly 56 million Americans (Identity Theft Resource Center, 2005). Moreover, in June of that same year it was reported that hackers had breached a network that handles merchant transactions, resulting in the loss of 40 million credit card numbers (Menn, 2005a,b). It is difficult to assess when and if victims of such personal information losses will be victimized through subsequent criminal activity, and thus whether they are adequately represented in either victim or general population surveys. Data collected over longer time periods would be required to assess the actual lag times before the discovery of criminal victimization. As an initial step, however, the ITRC should make greater efforts to collect comparable demographic data in the future so that more detailed comparisons with other survey results would be possible. Moreover, recent efforts to include new identity theft questions on the annual National Crime Victimization Survey in the United States must consider all of these issues as well.

Regarding some of the patterns of identity theft victimization reported here, decreases in time spent by victims resurrecting their identities (Table 10) might be evidence of social change in terms of awareness of victim services and institutional advances. However, the longer periods of crime engagement reported by victims might indicate that identity thieves have become more sophisticated in keeping their offenses hidden from victims, the authorities, and business. Familial identity theft is a significant problem for future study, as is child identity theft, which was reported more frequently in the 2004 ITRC survey. Information obtained in the ITRC surveys regarding the characteristics of identity thieves appears largely to coincide with more anecdotal information, especially in the areas of: organized crime; the link between drugs and identity theft; and the connection of such crimes to the misuse, theft, or loss of personal information in the business community.

As Newman (this volume) has noted, since " . . . identity theft is often composed of old crimes carried out in a new environment, it follows that many of the standard techniques of opportunity reduction should apply." Given the myriad ways in which identity information is obtained and used in criminal activities – including computer thefts, database breaches, or simply a lost or stolen wallet – situational crime prevention techniques will need to cover a much broader terrain than usual in order to be effective. Our preliminary analysis indicates a need for additional detailed research on these and related topics in order to better control future abuses.

Address correspondence to: hnpontel@uci.edu

NOTES

1. Staff noted that a few respondents were added who contacted the Center after October, and that these represented "extremely significant" cases.

2. Staff collected information from those who called for assistance to assure that they were in fact identity theft victims, and not persons who had other crime or personal information issues (e.g., a lost or stolen wallet). Persons whose identity theft cases had produced extreme psychological distress, whom staff determined to be in need of assistance by mental health professionals, were excluded from the original mailing list.

3. These and other findings are available at: www.consumer.gov/idtheft

4. Information presented at NIJ conference on identity theft, January 24, 2006, Washington, D.C.

5. Persons not included in this sample are those who simply lost personal information, or who thought that they may be victims, or who had experienced a theft or loss of a wallet or purse without having the personal information they contained subsequently used against them.

6. Comparisons to the 2003 survey are made where possible (since some questions on the 2004 survey were not included on the 2003 survey) and only where there are significant differences in responses.

7. The other three states in that top group were Nevada, Colorado and Arizona.

8. Regarding how their information was used by the identity thief, respondents could report multiple answers depending on all the ways in which the identity thief had used their personal data.

9. In total, 30% of respondents said that thieves had used checks in their names. Almost half of those responding reported that between one and nine checks were passed in their name.

10. The question stated that they should answer this only if it applies, but also gave a category "None." As the zero category was used for "none," and there was no option to answer "don't know" on the survey, we must assume that all responses that were coded zero include those who were not victimized in this manner and those who may not have known the number of cards. Thus the remaining responses probably underestimate the extent of the fraudulent use of new credit cards.

11. The question was confusing to some respondents, as some answered affirmatively, yet also checked unknown, since they may not have known the specific identity of the person who stole their information, but only that the person was "an employee," for example. Percentages were based on those who answered affirmatively, even if they had also checked the unknown category. Eleven percent of these respondents in 2004 did not provide an answer ("missing") compared to 18% in 2003. Given the question wording, some respondents answered more than once, so the percentages do not add up to 100.

12. Two survey questions were asked that attempted to gauge the amount of time victims had spent on their cases. One question asked how much time was spent if they considered the case closed, and the other the amount of time if they still considered it open. Respondents should have thus answered only one of these, but in some cases they answered both. Regardless of whether this was simply a matter of survey design and administration or confusion on the part of the respondents, since it is impossible to disentangle which question the respondents who answered both intended to answer, we have omitted them from the analysis. We found that 33 persons answered both questions in the 2004 survey, while 36 respondents did so in 2003. For these analyses we used only those respondents who answered one or the other question, and not both.

13. Persons who also answered that their cases were closed are excluded from these figures.

14. It should also be noted that reported time periods were given *at the time victims responded to the survey,* and thus do not distinguish those who are still being affected from those who are not. Thus, these responses must be taken as *conservative estimates since the assessment was made at this one point in time.* That is, some proportion of respondents has undoubtedly continued to be affected by their cases after the survey was conducted.

15. There is little correspondence between the 2004 and 2003 data, which may be due to the different coding schemes used by ITRC in the surveys and which could not be verified.

16. In total, 38% of respondents in 2004 and 47% in 2003 said that the company had promised to clear their records, but that the information remained on their credit reports for more than two months after that promise was made. Over 40% in both samples replied that the person who finally worked with them was a fraud investigator. Almost a quarter of the 2004 sample and about a third of the 2003 survey respondents said that the company told them that they had lost information that victims had submitted to them.

REFERENCES

Barkan, S.E. (2001). *Criminology: a sociological understanding,* 3rd ed. Upper Saddle River, NJ: Prentice Hall.

Baum, K. (2006). *Identity theft, 2004.* Washington, DC: U.S. Department of Justice, Bureau of Justice Statistics.

Catalano, S.M. (2004). *Criminal victimization, 2003.* Washington, DC: U.S. Department of Justice, Bureau of Justice Statistics.

Cole, S.A. and H.N. Pontell (2006). " 'Don't be low hanging fruit': Identity theft as moral panic." In T. Monahan (Ed.), *Surveillance and Security* (pp. 125-148). New York, NY: Routledge.

Colker, D. and J. Menn (2005, March 3). "ChoicePoint CEO had denied any previous breach of database." *Los Angeles Times,* pp. C1-C6.

Connell, S.A. (2004, August 29). "Students face possibility of identity theft." *Los Angeles Times,* p. B5.

Connelly, M. (1990, November 29). "Elderly victim of Lincoln S&L loss takes own life." *Los Angeles Times,* p. A1.

Cressey, D.R. (1953). *Other people's money: A study of the social psychology of embezzlement.* Glencoe, IL: Free Press.

Federal Trade Commission (2005). *National and state trends in fraud & identity theft: January – December 2004.* Washington, DC: author.

Identity Theft Resource Center (2005). *2005 disclosures of U.S. data fraud incidents.* Available at: http://www.tracesecurity.com/news/2005-data-disclosure.pdf

Klaus, P. (2004). *Crime and the nation's households, 2002.* Washington, DC: U.S. Department of Justice, Bureau of Justice Statistics.

Lemert, E.M. (1958). "The behavior of the systematic check forger." *Social Problems* 6(2):141-149.

Levi, M. (1992). "White collar crime victimization." In K. Schlegel and D. Weisburd (Eds.), *White-Collar Crime Reconsidered* (pp. 169-194). Boston, MA: Northeastern University Press.

Maguire, K. and A.L. Pastore (Eds.) (2004). *Sourcebook of criminal justice statistics 2002.* Available at: http://www.albany.edu/sourcebook.

Menn, J. (2005a, Feb. 16). "Fraud ring taps into credit data." *Los Angeles Times,* pp. A1-A20.

——— (2005b, June 18). "Hackers tap 40 million credit cards." *Los Angeles Times,* A1-A32.

Miethe, T.D. and R.F. Meier (1990). "Opportunity, choice, and criminal victimization: A test of a theoretical model." *Journal of Research in Crime and Delinquency* 27(3):243-266.

Needleman, M. and C. Needleman (1979). "Organizational crime: Two models of criminogenesis." *Sociological Quarterly* 20(4):517-39.

National Institute of Justice (2005, April). *Recommendations for research on identity theft.* Draft report. Washington, DC: author.

Newman, G.R. (2008). *Identity theft and opportunity.* (This volume.)

Newman, G.R. and M.M. McNally (2005). *Identity theft literature review.* Unpublished report prepared for the National Institute of Justice. Available at: http://www.ncjrs.gov/pdffiles1/nij/grants/210459.pdf

Rennison, C.M. (2003). *Intimate partner violence, 1993-2001.* Washington, DC: U.S. Department of Justice, Bureau of Justice Statistics.

Rennison, C.M. and M.R. Rand (2003). *Criminal victimization, 2002.* Washington, DC: U.S. Department of Justice, Bureau of Justice Statistics.

Rosoff, S.M., H.N. Pontell and R.H. Tillman (2007). *Profit without honor: White-collar crime and the looting of America,* 4th ed. Upper Saddle River, NJ: Prentice Hall.

Shichor, D., J.H. Doocy and G. Geis (1996). "Anger, disappointment and disgust: reactions of victims of a telephone investment scam." In C. Sumner, M. Israel, M. O'Connell and R. Sarre (Eds.), *International Victimology: Selected Papers from the 8th International Symposium* (pp. 105-112). Canberra, Australia: Australian Institute of Criminology.

Shichor, D., D.K. Sechrest and J. Doocy (2001). "Victims of investment fraud." In H.N. Pontell and D. Shichor (Eds.), *Contemporary issues in crime and criminal justice: Essays in honor of Gilbert Geis* (pp. 81-96). Upper Saddle River, NJ: Prentice Hall.

Shover, N., G.L. Fox and M. Mills (1994). "Long-term consequences of victimization by white-collar crime." *Justice Quarterly* 11(1):75-98.

Sullivan, B. (2004, June 14). *Criminals taking advantage of online banking, Gartner says.* MSNBC.com.

Synovate (2003). *Federal Trade Commission – Identity theft survey report.* Available at: http://www.ftc.gov/os/2003/09/synovatereport.pdf

Titus, R.M., F. Heinzelmann and J.M. Boyle (1995). "Victimization of persons by fraud." *Crime & Delinquency* 41(1):54-72.

van Kesteren, J., P. Mayhew and P. Nieuwbeerta (2001). *Criminal victimisation in seventeen industrialized countries: Key findings from the 2000 international crime victims survey.* The Hague, Netherlands: Netherlands Research and Documentation Centre.

THE RISKS, REWARDS AND STRATEGIES OF STEALING IDENTITIES[1]

by

Heith Copes

Department of Justice Sciences
University of Alabama at Birmingham

and

Lynne Vieraitis
Program in Criminology
University of Texas at Dallas

Abstract: *Despite the rapid rise in the occurrence of identity theft and the incredible costs to victims, little is known about the lifestyles and decision-making strategies of those who engage in this illegal enterprise. The purpose of this study is to examine identity theft from the offenders' perspectives. Drawing on semi-structured interviews with 59 offenders convicted of identity theft and incarcerated in federal prisons, this study describes how they account for their motivations, the risks they associate with the crime, the strategies they employ to locate sensitive information and convert it into cash, and the skills they have developed to be successful. Over all, the findings suggest that several well-known situational crime prevention techniques may be effective at reducing identity theft through increasing efforts, increasing risks, and removing excuses.*

Crime Prevention Studies, volume 23 (2008), pp. 87–110.

Fundamental shifts since World War II in the American economy, in communications technology and in public welfare functions of the state, are transforming crime. These changes have dramatically altered the opportunity structure of crime, and offenders have adapted accordingly. Whereas some crimes have dwindled in prevalence, others have boomed. The significant increase in economic crime evidences this point (Shover and Hochstetler, 2006). In the last ten years, one form of fraud – identity theft – has garnered America's attention as it became one of the most common economic crimes in the United States (Bernstein, 2004; Perl, 2003). According to recent data from the Federal Trade Commission, 685,000 complaints of fraud were reported in 2005; 37% of these complaints (255,565) were for identity theft (Federal Trade Commission, 2006). Considering that the average clearance rate for identity theft is around 11%, little is known about those engaging in the crime (Allison, Schuck and Lersch, 2005).

Despite the fact that identity theft is one of the fastest growing economic crimes in the United States, researchers have devoted little attention to understanding those who engage in this offense. Most importantly in this regard, there has yet to be a systematic examination of a sample of offenders. Such research could produce a more comprehensive picture of identity theft by assessing the viewpoints and "cognitive worlds" (Shover and Hochstetler, 2006) of offenders and, correspondingly, of how identity theft might be controlled more effectively. As such, this analysis explores offenders' perspectives through semi-structured interviews with a sample of incarcerated identity thieves. Specifically, the apparent rewards and risks they associate with identity theft, and the measures they employ to carry out their crimes, are examined. Suggestions are also offered for prevention and enforcement efforts with an improved potential for curbing identity theft.

METHODS

The present study is based on data collected from interviews with 59 inmates incarcerated in U.S. federal prisons for identity theft or identity theft-related crimes. A purposive sampling strategy was employed to locate federally convicted identity thieves, which involved an examination of newspapers and legal documents from across the United States. Lexis-Nexis News, an electronic database that organizes newspapers from around the United States by region and state, was used as the source for the newspapers. The Lexis-Nexis Legal Research database, containing decisions from all federal courts, and the Westlaw database, were also searched using the term "18 U.S.C. § 1028," which is the U.S. federal statute for identity theft. Finally, the websites of U.S. Attorneys in all 93 U.S. districts were searched for press releases and indictments regarding individuals charged with identity theft.

The online Federal Bureau of Prisons Inmate Locator (www.bop.gov) was then used to determine whether the offenders identified during the initial searches were currently being housed in federal facilities. In total, this process yielded the names of 297 identity thieves. Because it was not possible to interview all individuals, it was necessary to create a sample from this list. In order to solicit the participation of these inmates, visits were made to the 14 correctional facilities that housed the largest number of inmates in each of the six regions defined by the Federal Bureau of Prisons (Western, North Central, South Central, North Eastern, Mid-Atlantic, and South Eastern).

Semi-structured interviews were used to explore offenders' decision-making processes, with the goal of having them tell their stories in their own words. Although an attempt was made to ask all of the participants the same questions, this was not always possible. For example, questions pertaining to entering banks to cash checks were not applicable for those who engaged in mortgage fraud. Also, on several occasions participants would describe how they became involved in their crimes before all of the background questions could be asked. In these cases, such data were sought at the end of the interview so as not to disrupt the flow of the conversation regarding the details of the thefts and their perceptions of the crimes. When possible, interviews were audio-recorded and then transcribed verbatim. However, some wardens did not allow recording devices in their facilities, and some offenders would only agree to the interview if it was not recorded. To ensure inter-rater reliability, each transcript was independently read to identify common themes. The findings were then discussed with regard to identifying the overarching themes in these stories.

The final sample of 59 inmates included 23 men and 36 women. This discrepancy in gender is probably due to the sampling strategy and the higher response rate from female inmates. In addition, more males were unavailable for interviews because of their disciplinary problems. Offenders in the sample ranged in age from 23 to 60 years, with a mean age of 38 years. They included 18 white females, 16 African-American females, 2 Asian females, 8 white males, and 15 African-American males.

To gain an understanding of their life experiences, offenders were asked to describe their past and current family situations. Most offenders were currently or had been married in their lifetimes: 25% of the offenders were married, 31% were separated/divorced, 32% had never been married, and 5% were widowed. Approximately 75% of the offenders had children. With respect to educational achievement, the majority of offenders had at least some college.

Prior arrest patterns indicate that a large portion of the offenders had engaged in various types of offenses, including drug, property, and violent crimes. Yet, the majority of them claimed that they only committed identity thefts or comparable frauds (e.g., check fraud). In total, 37 of the offenders (63%) reported prior arrests, most of which were for financial fraud or identity theft (n = 26), but drug use/sales (n = 11) and property crimes (n = 13) were also relatively common.

Finally, inmates were questioned about their prior drug use. Approximately 58% (34 offenders) had tried drugs in their lifetime – mostly marijuana, cocaine in various forms, and methamphetamine. Only 22 reported having been addicted to their drug of choice. Of those offenders who said that they were using drugs while committing identity theft, only 14 reported that the drug use had contributed to their offense.

MOTIVES, REWARDS, AND JUSTIFICATIONS

Numerous studies of street-level property offenders and fraudsters find that the primary motivation for instigating these events is the need for money (Shover, 1996; Shover et al., 2004; Wright and Decker, 1994), and this was also true for the current sample of offenders. One of the offenders (Lawrence) probably best reflected this idea: "It's all about the money. That's all it's about. It's all about the money. If there ain't no money, it don't make sense." Indeed, identity theft can be richly and quickly rewarding. According to Lawrence: "I'll put it to you like this, forging checks, counterfeiting checks in an hour, depending on the proximity of the banks – the banks that you're working – I have made seven thousand dollars in one hour." Similarly, Gladys estimated that she could make "two thousand dollars in three days." These claims were consistent with those given by other offenders in the sample and with previous estimates in other research (Bureau of Justice Statistics, 2006).

While claims regarding how much they profited from their crimes varied widely among respondents, most brought in incomes greater than they could have earned from the types of legitimate work that they were qualified for or from other types of illegal enterprises. In fact, several of them described how they gave up other criminal endeavors for identity theft because they could make more money. When asked why she stopped selling drugs, Bridgette answered: "[Selling drugs is] not the answer. That's not where the money is." Dale switched from burglaries to identity theft arguing: "[Identity theft] is easier and you get the money, you know. You get a lot of money."

But how did they spend the money gained through their illegal enterprises? Identity thieves used the proceeds of their crimes to fund their chosen lifestyles. Of the 54 offenders for whom information was available, 23 led self-indulgent lifestyles (similar to persistent street offenders) that were characterized by the mentality of "life as party" (Jacobs and Wright, 1999; Shover and Honaker, 1992). Proceeds were more likely to be spent maintaining partying lifestyles filled with drug use and fast living, rather than putting money aside for long-term plans. Bridgette explained succinctly why she committed identity theft: "Getting money and getting high." This lifestyle was also described by Lawrence, "I made a lot of money and lost a lot of money. It comes in and you throw it out [on] partying and females. I gave a lot of money away. I bought a lot of things. A lot of people put things in their names. [I was going] back and forth to Miami to Atlanta. I mean it's a party . . . Just to party, go to clubs, strip clubs and stuff. Just to party." The ease at which money was made and spent was also reflected in the words of Carlos, "We're spending it pretty much as fast as we can get it, you know?"

However, not all indulged in such a lifestyle. In fact, some showed restraint in their spending. Nearly half of those for whom lifestyle information was available used their stolen money to support what would generally be considered a conventional life (n = 24). In addition, seven others could be seen as drifting between a party lifestyle and a more conventional one. These offenders made efforts to conceal their misdeeds from their friends and family and to present a law-abiding front to outsiders. They used the proceeds of identity theft to finance comfortable middle-class lives, including paying rent or mortgages, buying expensive vehicles, and splurging on the latest technological gadgets. When asked what he did with the money, Jake answered, "Nothing more than living off it, putting it away, saving it. Nothing flashy. Just living off it." Bruce engaged in identity theft "to maintain an upper class lifestyle. To be able to ride in first class, the best hotels, the best everything." Their lifestyles were also in line with the telemarketers interviewed by Shover et al. (2004). This is not to say that they did not indulge in the trappings of drugs and partying, as many did. As Denise explained: "I didn't do a lot of partying. I bought a lot of weed, paid out a lot, kept insurance going and the car note, put stereos in my car." Nevertheless, these offenders put forth an image of middle-class respectability.

In addition to the financial rewards of identity theft, there are intrinsic ones. As Jack Katz (1988) has explained, crime can be fun and exciting and 11 interviewees described identity theft in such a manner. These offenders said that they enjoyed the "adrenaline rush" experienced when entering banks and stores and by "getting over" on people. Cori explained, "It's just, it was, it was like a rush. . . . At first it was kind of fun. The lifestyle is addicting you know." When asked to describe the rush he felt from engaging in identity theft, Lawrence replied:

> It's money. It's knowing I'm getting over on them. Knowing I can manipulate the things and the person I got going in there. It's everything. It wasn't just . . . I guess you can say it is a little fear, but it's not fear for me, though. It's fear for the person I got going in there [accomplice entering bank]. I don't know. It's kind of weird. I don't know how to explain it but it's the rush. Knowing that I created this thing to manipulate these banks, you know what I'm saying? They're going to pay me for it and I'm going to manipulate this dude [bank teller] out of the money when they cashing those checks.

But even for these individuals, the thrill factor of identity theft was secondary to the money. Thrills alone did not appear to instigate or propel identity theft.

Previous reports on identity theft have pointed out that some of these crimes are precipitated by the desire to hide from the law or to get utilities or phone service activated (Newman, 2004). Only three people in the current sample mentioned such reasons. Jolyn, for example, had a warrant out for her arrest, so she used another's identity to get telephone service. While her crimes started as a means to get telephone services, she eventually used this information to garner social security benefits. Additionally, Jamie said, "I needed my utilities on. [I did it] for that reason. I've never used it as far as applying for a credit card though because I knew that was a 'no.' "

Although the financial benefits of their crimes are important, offenders must be able to make sense of their actions and maintain a positive self-image even when violating the law. While acknowledging that they needed money to support their lifestyles, participants would not engage in just any crime. They chose identity theft because they could more easily justify their actions (Sykes and Matza, 1957; Maruna and Copes, 2005). The most common way identity thieves justified their crimes was by denying that they caused any "real harm" to "actual individuals." It was not uncommon for identity thieves to make statements such as Fran's: "I always thought that just because it was white-collar crime it didn't hurt nobody," and Joel's, "Everything that I did was based on opening, grabbing the identity and then opening separate accounts. It affected them, but it was different." Many of them felt secure in their belief that stealing identities was only a minor hassle to victims, and that no real harm was caused because the victim could repair any credit damage with a few calls and, consequently, not suffer any direct financial loss. What this indicates is that these criminals draw on incorrect, yet common stereotypes regarding the "harmlessness" of white-collar crimes in order to neutralize their deviant behaviors. Thus, a direct connection between the social realities of white-collar and common crime exists in the social worlds of these offenders, and this is an important element in the justification of their crimes.

When identity thieves did acknowledge victims, they described them as large, "faceless" organizations that deserved victimization. Identity thieves argued that the only people who actually lose from their crimes are banks, corporations, or other victims who are thought not to deserve sympathy. Dustin confidently explained:

> I mean, like real identity theft, man, I can't do that. You know what I'm saying? Intentionally screw someone over, you follow what I'm saying? It's just, it's not right to me. So I couldn't do it. But corporations, banks, police departments, government – oh, yeah, let's go get 'em. Because that's the way they treat you, you know what I'm saying? If they done screwed me over, screw them.

When portraying victims as faceless or as "plastic," distancing oneself cognitively from the crime becomes remarkably easy.

Individuals who work within an organization to carry out their crimes sometimes rely on the diffusion of responsibility to excuse themselves. Although large amounts of money are eventually appropriated, many of the self-proclaimed low-level organizational members in the current sample claimed that they only played a minimal role in the crime; thus, by comparison, they should not be judged like the others. Additionally, these individuals pointed to the small amount of money they made as evidence that they "really didn't do anything." According to Lillian:

I never believed that I would be listed on the indictment. . . . I didn't go into it saying okay, I'm gonna make a ton of money off of this, you know? . . . When I saw the indictments and some of the amounts of the money that these folks were making, I mean 1.2 million dollars, you know. And I'm a struggling, just-out-of-school student. I lived in an apartment that was barely big enough for me, you know? My car was still owned by Mazda, you know what I mean? . . . Everybody I knew that worked in real estate as an attorney that's the kinda money they were making.

Jacob used a similar excuse: "I'm an outside guy. I'm not really involved. I don't know what's going on. I'm not making no transactions. None of this money is coming into any of my bank accounts. So I don't have nothing to do with it. But now I look like I'm the main guy."

Many identity thieves also seek to make sense of and justify their crimes by pointing out that their actions were done with noble intents – helping people. They set aside their better judgment because they thought their loyalties to friends and family were more important at that time. Betty explained, "And it's like I tell the judge, I regret what I had put my family through, but I don't regret at all what I did because everything that I did was for the safety of my kids. And I don't regret it. As a mother, I think you do whatever needs to [be done] to keep your kids safe."

PERCEPTIONS OF RISK

Interviews with persistent street offenders indicated that, for the most part, they do not dwell on the potential long-term legal risks of their endeavors (Shover and Honaker, 1992). Of the 40 participants who were asked directly if they thought about getting caught, 21 said they did not worry much about the possibility. When asked about being arrested, Penni replied: "Nope. I didn't care because I was good at what I did and I know I wasn't going to get caught." Similarly, Bradley responded, "Not really. I mean, I knew there was always a possibility, but that wasn't really on my mind. At the time I was just worried about getting money."

Offenders can be particularly adept at simply putting the consequences of their actions "out of mind" (Hochstetler and Copes, 2006). Many of the lawbreakers currently interviewed said that if thoughts of getting caught came up, they were pushed aside. They believed that dwelling on the risks of crime was detrimental to their success. Instead, they preferred to think positively and maintain an optimistic outlook when entering banks and stores for illicit purposes. Mindi explained: "When you get too comfortable doing illegal things, you become like, it's just like you get a superpower. You don't think you're going to get caught." Like athletes who enter competitive events with a mindset that they can and will win, identity thieves entered stores and banks with a mindset that they would be successful (Hochstetler and Copes, 2006).

Others who ignored the possibility of arrest and confinement believed that their advanced skills insulated them from being captured by law enforcement. By relying on their skills, they believed they could stay one step ahead of the law. According to Dustin: "It was calculated risk. Before the feds actually got me the first time, I never worried about getting caught. And that's the truth. I never worried about getting caught. Because that's how quick and good I was." When asked if he considered the risks, Carlos added, "Everything that we did was thought out very, very, very well and nothing was done cheaply."

Another reason identity thieves did not think about getting caught was because they saw their crimes as being easy. As Alisha explained: "I guess cause we were always up [from drug use] we never really thought too much about getting caught because we just knew it was easy." Similarly, Heidi stated: "Once you do it, I mean it's like, 'Whoa!' That was easy and fast."

Additionally, several of them stated that they did not think they would get caught because they had little faith in the ability of police. According to Lawrence: "Actually, the truth [is], I thought I was smarter than the police." He followed this up by saying, "Me, I thought all the police were stupid. Me, I thought they was all dumb." Those who relied on their skills to avoid detection and capture believed that the only way they would get caught was through bad luck, and this was the case for many of them. As Dale describes: "It's always bad luck that gets you caught. You don't get caught in the store; you don't get caught in the bank. I have never, since I been doing this, I've never been apprehended in the bank or department store."

Not all ignored the possibility of formal consequences. Of the 40 identity thieves who were asked about getting caught, 19 acknowledged that they would eventually lose their freedom due to their crimes. However, consistent with prior research on street offenders, they did not think they would be caught for the crime they were committing at the time (Feeney, 1986). For example, Sheila explained: "I looked at it like I'm not gonna get caught today, you know. I'm gonna make it through this one today."

Even though many knew they were eventually going to get caught, this belief had little deterrent effect on their choices. When assessing the costs and benefits of identity theft, offenders in the current sample were quick to mention the relatively low risk of detection and the minimal expectations of punishment associated with the crime. Many argued that since it was a "white-collar" crime, nothing severe would befall them if caught. When asked if she ever thought about getting caught Fran responded: "I did, but as I said, my mind frame was that it's white-collar crime. At that point in time, back then, everyone that was getting [convicted of] white-collar crime was getting a slap on the wrist." She was not alone in this belief. Mindi, an immigrant who was sentenced to 71 months, explained:

> I thought I was going to get caught. I did, but I didn't think it was going to be this big. I thought I was going to go to jail for a couple of months or something, not 71 months . . . [I thought] I would just pay for it for a little while and get out. Never in a million years I would think that all of [my family] would be deported and we lose everything, the cars, the houses. Nothing like this ever, ever crossed my mind!

According to Brandie: "I thought if we got caught we would possibly get – since I hadn't been in trouble before – something in my mind was still saying okay, probation you know, that's what I thought." When identity thieves conducted a mental cost benefit analysis of the crime, the belief that little harm would come to them coupled with the perceived high payoffs of the crime made it an attractive choice. These beliefs about sanctioning were based on stereotypes regarding the perceived lenient punishment of white-collar criminals who are more likely to be of higher class status, have legitimate occupations, and may thus have greater resources brought to bear on their legal defense. Identity thieves who perceive the consequences of their acts in this same light have severely underestimated their potential punishments.

METHODS AND TECHNIQUES OF IDENTITY THEFT

Acquiring Information

Offenders in this sample utilized a variety of methods to procure and convert information into cash and/or goods. In fact, most did not specialize in a single method, but preferred to use a number of strategies. Although 53% were employed at the time of their crimes, only 36% reported that their jobs facilitated the thefts. The majority of those who used their jobs to carry out their crimes committed mortgage fraud (n = 11). Others worked at government agencies (e.g., state departments of motor vehicles, n = 5) or businesses that had access to credit cards and social security numbers (n = 5). Few said that they sought employment for the purposes of easier access to sensitive information. In fact, several worked at jobs where they had access to identifying information but chose not to exploit their positions, preferring instead to steal identities elsewhere.

The most common method of obtaining a victim's information was to buy it (n = 13). Offenders in the current sample bought identities from employees of various businesses and state agencies who had access to personal information, such as names, addresses, dates of birth, and social security numbers (n = 5). Information was purchased from employees of banks, credit agencies, a state law enforcement agency, mortgage companies, departments of motor vehicles, hospitals, doctor's offices, a university, car dealerships, and furniture stores. Those buying information said that it was easy to find someone willing to sell them what they wanted. According to Gladys: "It's so easy to get information and everybody has a price." Penni said: " . . . people that work at a lot of places, they give you a lot of stuff – hospitals, DMV, like Wal-Mart, a lot of places, like (local phone company). People fill out applications a lot of stuff like that and you get it from a lot of people. There's a lot of tweekers (drug addicts) out there and everybody's trying to make a dollar and always trading something for something." When describing how she obtained information from a bank employee, Kristin said, "She was willing to make some money too, so she had the good information . . . that would allow me to have a copy of the signature card, passwords, work address, everything, everything that's legit."

Eight offenders who purchased information did so from persons they knew or who they were acquainted with "on the streets." Lawrence explained: "People [on the streets] knew what I was buying. I mean any city, there's always somebody buying some information." The identity thieves bought information from other offenders who obtained it from burglaries, thefts from motor vehicles, prostitution, and pickpocketing. One offender purchased information from boyfriends or girlfriends of the victims. For the most part, the current sample of offenders did not know nor care where their sellers obtained their information. As long as the information was good, they asked no questions.

Five individuals obtained information by using the "mailbox" method, and another two got information by searching through trashcans. These offenders typically stole mail from small businesses, such as insurance companies, or from residential mailboxes in front of homes or apartments. Some offenders simply drove through residential areas and pulled mail out, often taking steps to appear legitimate (e.g., they placed flyers advertising a business in mailboxes). Mailboxes and trashcans for businesses that send out mail with personal information (e.g., account numbers, social security numbers, and dates of birth) were also popular targets.

Although most of the offenders interviewed did not know their victims, of those who did, six said that the victim willingly gave them the information in exchange for a cut of the profits. In these cases, the "victim" gave the offender information to commit the identity theft and then reported that his or her identity had been stolen. Five offenders used family members' information without their knowledge, and in one case the information was for family members who were deceased. Another five stole from friends or acquaintances without their knowledge.

Other methods of acquiring victims' information included various thefts (e.g., house and car burglary, purse-snatching [n = 3]), and socially engineering people to get their information [n = 2]). One individual set up a fake employment site to get information from job applicants. Another used the birth announcements in newspapers to get the names of new parents and, posing as an insurance representative, called the parents to get information for "billing purposes." The offender made the phone calls from the waiting room of the hospitals where the infants were born so that the name of the hospital would appear on the victims' caller ID readouts. Another offender used rogue Internet sites to run background checks and order credit reports on potential victims. In addition, nine individuals claimed to work in a group where other co-offenders obtained information; these thieves chose not to ask where the information came from.

Converting Information

After obtaining a victim's information, the offender must convert that information into cash or goods. Most commonly, offenders used the information to acquire or produce additional identity-related documents, such as driver's licenses or state identification cards. Some offenders created the cards themselves with software and materials (e.g., paper and ink purchased at office supply stores or given to them by an employee of a state department of motor vehicles). Other offenders knew someone or had someone working for them who produced identification cards. Identification cards were needed to withdraw cash from the victim's existing bank account or to open a new account.

Offenders used a variety of methods to profit from stolen identities. The most common strategies were applying for credit cards in the victims' names (including major credit cards and department store credit cards), opening new bank accounts and depositing counterfeit checks, withdrawing money from existing bank accounts, applying for loans, and applying for public assistance programs. Identity thieves often used more than one technique when cashing in on their crimes.

The most common strategy for converting stolen identities into cash was applying for credit cards. In total, 23 offenders used the information to order new credit cards. In a few cases, the information was used to get the credit card agency to issue a duplicate card on an existing account. Offenders used credit cards to buy merchandise for their own personal use, to resell the merchandise to friends and/or acquaintances, or to return the merchandise for cash. Offenders also cashed the checks that are routinely sent to credit card holders by credit card companies. Offenders also applied for store credit cards such as department stores and home improvement stores. According to Emma:

> [I would] go to different department stores, most often it was Lowe's or Home Depot, go in, fill out an application with all the information, and then receive instant credit in the amount from say $1,500 to $7,500. Every store is different. Every individual is different. And then at that time, I would purchase as much as that balance that I could at one time. So if it was $2,500, I would buy $2,500 worth of merchandise.

Another common strategy was to produce counterfeit checks. Sixteen offenders either made fraudulent checks on their own or knew someone who would produce these checks for them. Although most offenders who counterfeited checks produced personal checks, others made insurance company checks or payroll checks. They cashed these checks at grocery stores, purchased merchandise, and paid bills to companies such as utilities or cell phone vendors.

Sometimes identity thieves would use the stolen identities to open either a new bank account as a way to deposit fraudulent checks or to withdraw money from an existing account. Sixteen of the people interviewed reporting using this strategy, which required that the offender have information about the victim's bank account.

Another method of conversion included applying for and receiving loans; 14 individuals used this strategy. The majority of those who applied for loans engaged in some type of mortgage fraud. These types of scams often involved using victim's information to purchase homes for themselves. In one case, the offenders were buying houses and then renting them for a profit. Others applied for various auto loans, home equity loans, or personal loans.

SKILLS

As with any behavior, skills improve with experience. With practice, persistent burglars learn to assess the risks and value of homes almost instantaneously, crack dealers and prostitutes learn to discern undercover officers, and hustlers learn to recognize potential "marks" (targets for scams). Identity thieves have also developed a skill set to successfully accomplish their crimes. Four broad categories of skills emerged from the current analysis: (1) social skills, (2) intuitive skills, (3) technical skills, and (4) system knowledge.

Identity thieves claimed that having good social skills was an important quality to possess. This implies that they consider the ability to manipulate the social situation through verbal and non-verbal communication as a significant skill. For example, in order to be successful, an identity thief must possess the ability to "pass" as a regular customer in stores and banks, and to accurately and easily represent the person they claim to be. This ability allows identity thieves to construct a larcenous situation as real, thereby removing any doubts about the legitimacy of the interactions involved. Identity thieves accomplish this through dress, mannerisms and speech.

When questioned as to what makes her a "good" identity thief, Gladys responded: "I mean I can go into a place . . . knowing how to look the part in certain situations. . . . You go up to a place and you look in there and get the feeling about how a person would look and I'd take off a ring or something, put on a ring, take off some make-up, or go put on a hat or a scarf, put some glasses on." Tameka also "dressed" the part: "I might have on a nurse uniform." In describing what it was like interacting with bank and store employees, Bruce, an experienced thief, said: "You definitely have to be adaptable. It's not even being pleasant with people. It's just having authority. You have to have authority of whatever situation you are in. And if you have that authority, people will not go any further than to peripherally question you. That's about it."

A second skill that identity thieves develop is intuition, which can be defined as "an acute sensitization to and awareness of one's external surrounding" (Faupel, 1986). The ability to recognize criminal opportunity, sense danger, and know when to call off a criminal plan has been referred to as "larceny sense," "grift sense," and "intuitive sense" (Faupel, 1986; Maurer, 1951; Sutherland, 1937). Some offenders believed superstitiously that they had developed the ability to sense trouble: if they did not "feel bad" about a crime, then they felt they were safe. Regarding the ability to sense trouble, April noted: "You kind of get, I don't know, almost like you dreaded walking into it." When asked how he got better at identity theft, Bruce responded:

> Sensing . . . sensing what was going on within a situation, like at a bank, like I could sense what was going on with tellers. I could tell how they were looking at the screen, how long they were looking at it and I could sense whether something had been written or if I was cashing too many checks. Just a sense of how people react in situations and then also just the situations themselves. As many as they presented themselves, I would find a way around them. So I guess just honing the thinking on your feet . . . in the situations that came up.

Several offenders in this study believed they would not have been caught if they had paid better attention to their premonitions. For instance, Kimi described the moments before she was arrested:

> I knew the detectives were watching. I knew that and I had the feeling and I told [my co-defendant] but he was trying to kick heroin that day. And this stupid fool was shooting [heroin] and I'm all surrounded by heroin addicts . . . and I told him I said, we got to leave. I have this freaking feeling something's going to go wrong.

Whether or not repeat offenders have a heightened ability to sense danger is less important than the fact that many believe they do.

A third type of skill identity thieves develop involves the technical knowledge needed to produce fraudulent documents such as identification, checks, and credit applications. Making these documents look real is an increasingly difficult task. For example, determining the right type of paper to print checks on, how to replicate watermarks, and matching the colors on drivers' licenses are necessary skills that must be learned. Lawrence described this aspect: "I use a different type of paper. I use a regular document. The paper always came straight from the bank. A lot of people, they would get paper out of like, Target or Office Max, or places like that.

That kind of paper right there, it's not always sufficient. Nine times out of ten, the bank may stop it. They want to check the company payroll." While many identity thieves contract out for their documents, a sizable number learn these tricks through experimentation and practice. Kimi described her process:

> We studied IDs then I went to the stamp shop, the paint shop, got the logos right and I know the [Bank] was one of the hardest banks for us to get money out, but when I found out about the logos, when I passed it through the black light, it became real easy....I went to the stamp shop and bought a stamp and sat there for hours and hours with the colors and I made like seven different IDs before it come through under the black light.

The final skill discussed by identity thieves is system knowledge. This involves understanding how banks and credit agencies operate and knowing which stores require identification when cashing checks. According to Carlos:

> Well you definitely have to know how loans work. You have to know how title companies work, funding companies, banks in general. Then on top of that you have to be pretty adept with computers, how to, you know, pull a program apart. And I don't mean in code, but how to really operate a program. And that goes with anything you gotta know how all of that works. . . . So yeah there's some skills you definitely have to have and you really gotta know the rules, you know. I think that's a lot of what people don't really get is that it's, it's easier, everything is easier than you think if you know the rules, you know?

Echoing this, Sherry explained: "You have to have an idea of how banks work. At some point in your life, live a normal life and understand how credit is extended and things like that."

The development of these various skills plays an important role in crime persistence. By developing these skills, identity thieves increase their chances of being successful at crime; that is, these skills allow them to avoid the formal sanctions associated with identity theft. Those who commit crime with impunity have overly optimistic views of their crimes (Cusson, 1993; Paternoster et al., 1982), which was the case for many of those that were interviewed. Offenders came to believe that they could continue offending because they could rely on their skills to evade sanctions, thereby nullifying the deterrent effects of criminal sanctions.

POLICY IMPLICATIONS

All crime-control programs build upon assumptions about the nature of the target crime and the typical characteristics of those who commit it. In the best of circumstances, this knowledge is based on systematic data collection and analysis of offenders' accounts. Some have suggested, in fact, that "[t]here can be no more critical element in understanding and ultimately preventing crime than understanding the criminal's perceptions, opportunities and risks associated with (the type of crime in question)" (Rengert and Wasilchick, 1989:1). The policy implications included here are based on data collected from the current offender sample, and may therefore only be applicable to this group. In particular, they may not apply to offenders who are more professional, have different belief systems, or who engage in different types of identity theft. Although the extent to which this group of offenders represents either identity thieves or the phenomenon of identity theft is unknown, they do represent some or possibly most of them.

Law enforcement can and has made it more difficult for offenders to acquire information by encouraging the public to protect sensitive information. However, businesses and agencies may have the greatest potential for preventing active and potential identity thieves from acquiring information and converting it to cash and/or goods. In the following section, a set of policy suggestions for preventative efforts to reduce identity theft is outlined based on how identity thieves discuss their crimes. These suggestions incorporate several well-known situational crime prevention techniques, including increasing the effort an offender must use to acquire and convert information, increasing the risks of getting caught, removing excuses that may be used to justify their crime, and changing offenders' perceptions of punishment.

Increasing the Effort and Risks

The situations where identity thieves are most exposed to law enforcement are (1) getting the appropriate information and (2) entering banks or stores to cash in on the crime. Much has already been done to make it more difficult for thieves to secure information. Media campaigns warning citizens to guard their personal information have been widespread. These campaigns typically focus on telling people to protect their information. The findings of the current research support these attempts to reduce identity theft, at least for the opportunistic offender.

In addition to target hardening efforts on the part of individuals, the interviews suggest that businesses can play an important part in preventing offenders from acquiring information. The techniques for preventing identity theft outlined in Newman and McNally (2005:70) likely would have prevented many of the offenders in our sample from acquiring information. For example, a number of offenders stole information from the mailboxes or dumpsters of small businesses. Controlling access to these targets or monitoring how documents are disposed of (e.g., shredding documents with identifying information) would have restricted the number of areas from which offenders got their information. Programs designed to educate potential victims and any measures for controlling access to information will be ineffective, however, when information is compromised by individuals who have legitimate access to this data.

Many of the offenders in the current sample were able to purchase information from employees of various businesses and agencies. Organizations whose employees have access to personal information must therefore take steps to reduce the likelihood that identity thieves can acquire this information from employees. Such strategies may include: limiting the number of employees with access to the information, careful background checks of employees, maintaining a positive work environment, and alerting employees to the serious consequences of identity theft for both victims and perpetrators.

While most crime reduction strategies focus on preventing the acquisition of information by encouraging individuals and businesses to protect their information, this is not the only, or even the most effective, strategy. Overwhelmingly, the thieves who were interviewed said that entering banks and stores was seen as the riskiest part of the crime. Thus, this may be the most effective stage in the criminal event on which to focus prevention efforts. Banks could make simple changes in procedures that would increase the effort and risk of identity theft. For instance, they could require passwords to withdraw money from accounts or cash checks, even when customers engage in these transactions in person. Several of the offenders suggested that had this been in place, they could not have completed their withdrawals. Because the majority of offenders in the current sample obtained personal and banking information from strangers, it would be very difficult if not impossible for them to guess their victims' passwords. This strategy would clearly not deter thieves who have inside partners or who gain access to the bank's computer system, but these types of identity theft are rare.

Bank employees should also be more aware of who enters the bank. Identity thieves often hire "writers" to go into the bank to cash the checks or withdraw money. Because writers cannot be trusted, the "ring leader" often escorts them to the bank. Security should be aware of individuals who are dropped off or who walk to the bank. Simply looking for certain types of people will prove to be ineffective, however, because identity thieves have learned to dress and act the part when entering banks. Thus, security should watch for behaviors and not people.

Stores should require identification when customers pay by checks or credit cards. While many identity thieves produce fake identification, not all have the capability of doing so effectively. For this strategy to be effective, it is necessary for all stores to be consistent in checking identification. With experience and inside knowledge, identity thieves learn which stores check identification and what dollar amounts require proof of identification or manager approval. If some stores do not follow these policies, then target displacement is likely to occur (Clarke, 1983). The problem with many antitheft programs is that, "Within easy reach of every house with a burglar alarm, or car with an antitheft device, are many others without such protection" (Clarke, 1983:246). Thus, it is necessary that all stores require proof of identification; otherwise, there will be too many suitable targets within easy reach of offenders and the deterrent effect of the program will be undercut.

Removing Excuses

Situational crime prevention programs have been developed to counteract the "neutralization" techniques of potential offenders. The theory is that by learning the linguistic devices that offenders use to make their crimes palatable to themselves, program designers can attack these belief systems. By "neutralizing the neutralizations," offenders would not be able to define their actions as non-criminal, and thus would refrain from criminal behavior (Clarke, 1997; Clarke and Homel, 1997; Copes and Williams, 2007). True to the roots of situational crime prevention, "removing excuses" in this way does not entail making long-term changes in the prospective offender's personal dispositions, as do cognitive-based programs in correctional settings. Instead, situational crime prevention theorists argue that programs geared toward removing excuses should still focus on highly specific forms of crime and should be presented at the time criminal decisions are being made. The idea is to "stimulate feelings of conscience at the point of contemplating the commission of a specific kind of offense" (Clarke, 1997:24).

Researchers have suggested numerous programs to help reduce crime based on the premise of removing of excuses. Thurman et al. (1984) found that neutralizations used to justify tax evasion can block the potential inhibiting effects of guilt. They suggest that campaigns designed to make tax cheaters feel guilty about their behaviors can reduce the prevalence of tax fraud. Most commonly, though, these interventions are targeted to stop deviant behavior that occurs within formal organizations, such as workplaces and schools (Pelfrey, 1984; Greenberg, 1990; Lim, 2002). For instance, organizational managers are encouraged to openly discuss the neutralizations that wayward employees use. Bringing these neutralizations into the open is thought to force employees to consciously consider their actions when stealing from the company (Cressey, 1953).

These principles can be applied to identity theft. For this approach to work, it is necessary to present the anti-neutralization message at the immediate situation of the crime. While this may prove difficult for identity theft, there are ways it can be accomplished successfully. A large proportion of the identity thefts described by participants required them to go into banks to cash checks or withdraw funds. It is here that messages could be placed reminding offenders that their actions harm individuals. The goal is to make potential offenders recognize the harm they are doing in those locations where they carry out their crimes. Publicity campaigns similar to those used to deter movie piracy and cable theft could be implemented for identity theft. The best locations for these campaigns include banks, retail stores, and any other location where thieves must go to convert stolen identities into cash or merchandise.

A large percentage of identity thieves also obtained the information they needed to carry out their crimes from people who had legitimate access to this information. Thus, dishonest employees play a large role in the prevalence of identity theft. The "remove excuses" campaigns would also serve to educate employees who might be tempted to misuse their position to illegally sell sensitive information to others (Lim, 2002; Pelfrey, 1984).

Advertise Consequences

Identity thieves repeatedly made reference to their expectations of lenient punishment if they did happen to be apprehended. With the promise of large rewards with relatively little effort and perceptions of inconsequential punishments, it is easy to understand why they chose to commit identity theft. But the actual punishments these offenders received typically exceeded their expectations. Instead of being given probation or a year of incarceration, they were given sentences ranging from 12 to 360 months. Lawrence, who was sentenced to three years, stated: "I ain't knew they'd give me this much time. I thought because of a white-collar crime I'd get a slap on the wrist and like probation or something." Bradley, who was sentenced to 12 months said; "So I figured the worst I could get was probation. You know because I wasn't doing like hundreds of thousands of dollars."

The underestimates of potential sentences likely contributed to their habituation of identity theft. It is therefore likely that educating potential thieves about the true consequences of being convicted, at least at the federal level, could persuade them to desist. It is always a difficult task to educate target populations about the costs of crime, but it is possible. Evidence shows that significant reductions in homicide and gun violence were achieved by implementing a "lever-pulling" strategy involving face-to-face communication of a deterrence message (McGarrell et al., 2006; Kennedy, 1998). Similar programs could be implemented to target both chronic identity thieves and the larger population. Following principles of situational crime prevention, these deterrent messages can also be delivered at the scene of the crime. Just as messages informing offenders of the real harm they cause can be presented at the locations of the crimes, so too can these deterrent messages.

Decades of deterrence research have shown that perceived punishments have a greater deterrent effect than actual punishments, and it is necessary to change the perceptions of punishment held by identity thieves. Campaigns designed to create the impression that law enforcement agencies consider identity theft to be a serious crime, and that cases will be prosecuted to their fullest extent, may go a long way in changing offender perceptions about this offense. If successful, these informational campaigns would likely reduce identity theft. Although there is disagreement about the effectiveness of publicity campaigns (Mazerolle, 2003), " . . . publicity campaigns may represent a powerful yet cost-effective tool in crime prevention" (Johnson and Bowers, 2003:497) if properly planned.

✦

Address correspondence to: Heith Copes, University of Alabama at Birmingham, Department of Justice Sciences, 1201 University Blvd; Suite 210, Birmingham, AL 35294; e-mail: jhcopes@uab.edu

NOTES

1. This project was supported by Grant No. 2005-IJ-CX-0012 awarded by the National Institute of Justice, Office of Justice Programs, U.S. Department of Justice. Points of view in this document are those of the authors and do not necessarily represent the official position or policies of the U.S. Department of Justice. We thank the editors of the volume, Michael Cherbonneau, Kent Kerley, and Henry Pontell for their comments on an earlier draft.

REFERENCES

Allison, S., A. Schuck, and K. M. Lersch (2005). "Exploring the crime of identity theft: Prevalence, clearance rates, and victim/offender characteristics." *Journal of Criminal Justice* 33:19-29.

Bernstein, S. E. (2004). "New privacy concern for employee benefit plans: combating identity theft." *Compensation and Benefits Review* 36:65-68.

Bureau of Justice Statistics (2006). *Identity theft, 2004* (NCJ 212213). Washington, DC: author.

Clarke, R. V. (1983). "Situational crime prevention: Its theoretical basis and practical scope." In: M. Tonry and N. Morris (Eds.), *Crime and Justice: An Annual Review of Research*. Chicago, IL: University of Chicago Press.

Clarke, R.V. (1997). *Situational crime prevention: Successful case studies* (2nd Ed.). Monsey, NY: Criminal Justice Press.

Clarke, R.V. and R. Homel (1997). "A revised classification of situational crime prevention techniques." In S. P. Lab (Ed.), *Crime Prevention at a Crossroads*. Cincinnati, OH: Anderson.

Copes, H. and P. Williams (2007). "Techniques of affirmation: deviant behavior, moral commitment, and resistant subcultural identity." *Deviant Behavior* 28:247-272.

Cressey, D. R. (1953). *Other people's money: A study in the social psychology of embezzlement*. Glencoe, IL: Free Press.

Cusson, M. (1993). "Situational deterrence: Fear during the criminal event." In: R. Clarke (Ed.), *Crime Prevention Studies*, vol. 1. Monsey, NY: Criminal Justice Press.

Faupel, C.E. (1986). "Heroin use, street crime, and the 'main hustle': implications for the validity of official crime data." *Deviant Behavior* 7:31-45.

Federal Trade Commission (2006). *Consumer fraud and identity theft complaint data, January – December 2005*. Washington, DC: author.

Feeney, F. (1986). "Robbers as decision makers." In D. Cornish and R. Clarke (Eds.), *The Reasoning Criminal: Rational Choice Perspectives on Offending*. New York, NY: Springer-Verlag.

Gibson, K. (2000). "Excuses, excuses: Moral slippage in the workplace." *Business Horizons*, November/December:65-72.

Greenberg, J. (1990). "Employee theft as a reaction to underpayment inequity: The hidden cost of pay cuts." *Journal of Applied Psychology* 75:561–68.

Hochstetler, A. and H. Copes (2006). "Managing fear to commit felony theft." In P. Cromwell (Ed.), *In Their Own Words: Criminals on Crime*. Los Angeles, CA: Roxbury.

Jacobs, B. and R. Wright (1999). "Stick-up, street culture, and offender motivation." *Criminology* 37:149-73.

Johnson, S.D. and K.J. Bowers (2003). "Opportunity is in the eye of the beholder: The role of publicity in crime prevention." *Criminology and Public Policy* 2:497-524.

Katz, J. (1988). *Seductions of crime*. New York, NY: Basic Books.

Kennedy, D. (1998). "Pulling levers: Getting deterrence right." *National Institute of Justice Journal* 236:2-8.

Lim, Vivien K.G. (2002). "The IT way of loafing on the job: Cyberloafing, neutralizing and organizational justice." *Journal of Organizational Behavior* 23:675–94.

Maruna, S. and H. Copes (2005). "What have we learned from fifty years of neutralization research?" *Crime and Justice: A Review of Research* 32:221-320.

Maurer, D.W. (1951). *Whiz mob: A correlation of the technical argot of pickpockets with their behavior patterns*. Gainesville, FL: American Dialect Society.

Mazerolle, L. (2003). "The pros and cons of publicity campaigns as a crime control tactic." *Criminology and Public Policy* 2:531-540.

McGarrell, E.F., S. Chermak, J.M. Wilson and N. Corsaro (2006). "Reducing homicide through a 'lever-pulling' strategy." *Justice Quarterly* 23:214-231.

Newman, G.R. (2004). *Identity theft*. Washington, DC: U.S. Department of Justice.

Newman, G.R. and M.M. McNally (2005). *Identity theft literature review*. Paper presented at the National Institute of Justice focus group meeting. Available at: http://www.ncjrs.gov/pdffiles1/nij/grants/210459.pdf

Paternoster, R., L. Saltzman, T. Chiricos and G. Waldo (1982). "Perceived risk and deterrence: methodological artifacts in perceptual deterrence research." *Journal of Criminal Law and Criminology* 73:1238-1258.

Pelfrey, W.V. (1984). "Keep honest employees honest." *Security Management* 6:22–24.

Perl, Michael W. (2003). "It's not always about the money: Why the state identity theft laws fail to address criminal record identity theft." *Journal of Criminal Law and Criminology* 94:169-208.

Rengert, G. and J. Wasilchick (1989). *Space, time and crime: Ethnographic insights into residential burglary*. Final Report to the National Institute of Justice. Washington, DC: U.S. Department of Justice.

Shover, N. (1996). *Great pretenders: Pursuits and careers of persistent thieves*. Boulder, CO: Westview.

Shover, N., G. Coffey and C. Sanders (2004). "Dialing for dollars: Opportunities, justifications and telemarketing fraud." *Qualitative Sociology* 27:59-75.

Shover, N. and A. Hochstetler (2006). *Choosing white-collar crime*. New York: Cambridge University Press.

Shover, N. and D. Honaker (1992). "The socially bounded decision making of persistent property offenders." *Howard Journal of Criminal Justice* 31:276-93.

Sutherland, E. (1937). *The professional thief*. Chicago, IL University of Chicago Press.

Sykes, G. and D. Matza (1957). "Techniques of neutralization: A theory of delinquency." *American Sociological Review* 22:664–70.

Thurman, Q. C., C. S. John and L. Riggs (1984). "Neutralizations and tax evasion: How effective would a moral appeal be in improving compliance to tax laws?" *Law and Policy* 6:309-28.

Wright, R. and S. Decker (1994). *Burglars on the job*. Boston, MA: Northeastern University Press.

COMBATING IDENTITY AND OTHER FORMS OF PAYMENT FRAUD IN THE UK: AN ANALYTICAL HISTORY

by

Michael Levi
School of Social Sciences
Cardiff University

Abstract: *This chapter presents a history of the UK's efforts to combat check and payment card fraud. Some consideration is also given fraud prevention in the international context. Since the 1980s, the focus of preventive efforts has shifted from lost and stolen plastic cards to card-not-present transactions. This shift largely reflects industry controls, which have reduced conventional opportunities for plastic card crime. The discussion traces the history of control efforts and their relationship to fraud rates, as well as the evolution of "card fraud" to "identity fraud." Over all, the UK's experience provides one example of how opportunities for fraud can be reduced, though each country has a different alignment of commercial interests that affect the economic and logistical difficulties of change.*

This paper offers a history of the UK's efforts to combat check and payment card fraud since the 1980s, based on the author's involvement in periodic research projects on these crimes and their control. Although the analysis is focused primarily on the UK, the Internet and cheap international travel have transformed the role of the nation-state as a natural boundary both for fraud prevention and – to a lesser extent because of legal and procedural inhibitions – for criminal justice interventions, so the evidence and control measures are placed in international context. It will be observed that the evolution of "the problem" over the past 15 years has led to a shift in emphasis from conventional frauds on lost and stolen cards (obtained in transit to cardholders and directly from them or their property) to the late modern form of crimes-at-a-distance in the shape of Card Not Present (CNP) fraud.

Chiming with populist media and political concerns, nowadays *all* plastic fraud is included within "identity fraud" (see Home Office, 2006) in ways that are not particularly helpful for clarity of problem definition, as discussed later in this paper. This replacement by Card Not Present fraud is not an automatic or historically inevitable. Rather, it reflects the ways in which the industry, responding to evidence on absolute levels of fraud and rising forms thereof (Levi et al., 1991; Levi and Handley, 1998; Webb, 1996), has instituted controls that have reduced conventional card crime opportunities that were the softest targets with the largest share of losses before the 21st century. Thus, even if CNP fraud had not risen in absolute terms – which it has done – it would have risen as a *proportion* of plastic fraud as other types fell in absolute terms.

Each country has its own pattern of organization of the card business, and tensions vary between card issuers, acquirers (who receive fees in exchange for early reimbursement to merchants of their card transactions), merchants, card schemes (principally Visa, MasterCard, and American Express), cardholders and governmental regulators. This pattern of organization (and its corresponding economic interests), plus the energy and imagination of anti-fraud entrepreneurs, shapes the nature of the measures that are taken and the speed of their implementation. These patterns of control are not fixed over time and space, however, and the UK experience is instructive as a view of how opportunities to defraud can be reduced.

A BRIEF HISTORY OF CONTROL EFFORTS AND THEIR RELATIONSHIP WITH FRAUD RATES

There is an interactive relationship between control measures and fraud rates. It is usual for senior executives to require evidence of alarming growth in fraud before they invest resources in change, especially (inter-viewees state) if that investment will involve significant expenditure in the short run and the benefits will materialize only some years later, after their likely departure. This hypothesis may not be universal, and it is a challenge to the theory of the firm in conventional economics: one might expect to see greater willingness to invest in fraud prevention where senior executives had longer tenure and investors were more oriented to the long-term interests of the companies.[1] However, following is a history of payment card fraud in the UK and its control (data supplied by the Association for Payment Clearing Services [APACS]):

- 1988 (fraud loss £69.3 million) – The opening up of banks to increased competition led to a fight for market share and it significantly reduced income, alongside higher costs. This resulted in the card industry going for business growth, without adequate consideration of fraud risks.

- 1990 – A study was conducted on the prevention of check and plastic fraud, commissioned by the Home Office (Levi et al., 1991).

- 1990/92 (1992 fraud loss of £165 million was at that time a record high) – Home Office put pressure on the card industry, using the report by Levi et al. (1991), which focused the industry on cooperation and data-sharing measures, rejecting as a cost-(in)effective solution the then popular notion that photographs on cards would be the best way of cutting out card crime.[2] Recommendations were also directed to police and retailers, as well as the card schemes to monitor fraudu-lent merchants.

- 1992/95 (fraud loss in 1995 was £83.3 million, less than half of 1992 figure) – A concerted effort by the card industry was directed at short- and long-term solutions. The short-term efforts asked, inter alia, for partnership with retailers (at the cost of the card industry, since it impacted on the retailer), and the introduction of measures aimed at "card not received" (by the cardholder) cases – some components of which were aimed at theft from the mails. These resulted in the reduc-tion in fraud, which is even more significant in the context of rising volumes of card use.

- 1995/99 – Small rises in losses were seen until 1999, when a steeper rise of 40% occurred. Levi and Handley (1998) called for further action, including action against "card not present" (CNP) frauds.

- Figure 1 can best illustrate the migration from lost and stolen cards to more organized areas of payment card crime – mainly counterfeiting

Figure 1: Migration of Plastic Card Fraud.

Source: Association for Payment Clearing Services (APACS).

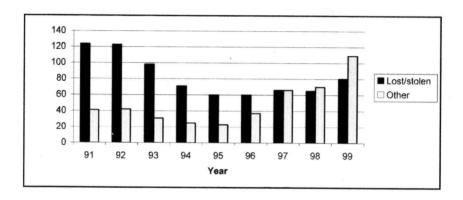

and CNP incidents. The pattern of fraud in the early 1990s required a crime reduction approach directed at the thief/fraudster who stole a credit (or, more rarely at that time, a debit) card, but the pattern shifted towards greater technological sophistication and wider networking to take advantage of "skimming": i.e., the copying of data on the magnetic stripe onto other cards, whether embossed or mere "white cards" that could be used in remote terminals.

The Reasons for the Rises

- Although short-term control efforts were a great success, the shift in fraudulent activity to CNP incidents required longer-term measures such as the introduction of a card authentication method (a "smart" card which enables the "reader" to check whether the card is genuine and not counterfeited),[3] the introduction of a cardholder verification method (CVM) that was more effective than the signature to verify whether the card-presenter was the legitimate cardholder, and also enhanced technology to authorize telephone and Internet transactions.

- Although some firms had begun to consider the generic business case for smart cards (to impact on skimming and counterfeit losses), the need for widespread introduction – given the need for the card use controls of Chip and PIN (see next section) to work in most terminals

– required general industry agreement on the issue. Furthermore, their rollout was delayed by arguments over who paid for the introduction of smart card readers at the retail-owned (rather than bank-owned) point of sale. The French smart card system with PIN had been in place in the 1970s, but its introduction and universality was facilitated by the near total control exercised by Carte Bleu,[4] which was not present in the UK market.

- Criminals used numbers obtained from cardholders by skimming, shouldering, etc., from card vouchers with cardholder details or from web sites such as CreditMaster (not to be confused with the legitimate credit solutions business of that name), which served no obvious legitimate purpose. In the absence of Chip and PIN, there was little at this time to protect the payment system against this type of fraud. Fraudsters purported to be retailers to collect card information and hackers did not present the same level of threat as the above.

THE BIRTH OF CHIP AND PIN

The assumption is often made in crime prevention that there is some cool rationality, even inevitability, in the changes that are made. However, as in this Chip and PIN case,[5] change often needs to be driven through by the passionate commitment of key individuals, without which the "rationality" will not materialize.[6] Having won agreement in principle to its introduction to meet the fast-growing threat of counterfeiting/skimming – to which the banking system had no technological answer – a three-month Chip and PIN trial started in Northampton in May 2003. This area was selected partly because it is demographically representative of the UK as a whole and partly because it is conveniently the home of Barclaycard, the largest UK card issuer and one of the key drivers of this change.

By the end of the trial, more than 200,000 PIN-enabled credit and debit cards had been issued: 1,000 outlets, including shops, restaurants, pubs, hotels and petrol stations had taken part, and over 170,000 Chip and PIN transactions had taken place. To replicate the gradual switch-on of the national rollout, some stores were not upgraded and many customers continued to use signatures. Stimulated by the banking industry, the scheme was given massive publicity that highlighted its card fraud reduction aspects.

Market research among Northampton consumers three months into the trial (July 2003) showed that 89% were aware of Chip and PIN, and

83% were in favor of its introduction. Two-thirds of Northampton's Chip and PIN cardholders felt that the cards were safer. Remembering a PIN was also proving to be less of a problem than anticipated: 97% of respondents knew the PIN on their debit card and 67% knew the PIN on their credit cards. On the other hand, though less stressed in the banking industry's public relations materials, this meant that a third of credit card users did *not* know their PIN, at least at that time.

Following the successful trial, the national rollout of Chip and PIN began in October 2003. This involved upgrading more than 860,000 shop terminals and 40,000 cash machines, issuing 140 million credit and debit cards to 42 million customers, and training over 3 million staff (many in businesses with high turnover of staff, so this generated some ongoing retraining issues). By early 2005, 45% of those questioned said they were already using Chip and PIN for all or most of their card payments and 97% of active cardholders knew about Chip and PIN. Eight of ten Chip and PIN debit cardholders were "very confident" about entering their PIN at the till.

How was this achieved? It happened largely (after significant internal skirmishing) because the card industry agreed to pay for retail implementation. (The retailers, appreciating that the card industry had already invested huge sums, realized that they had a strong bargaining position: if the card industry refused to pay for retail costs, this investment would have been largely wasted.) The effect was clear: reduced losses from card-present fraud, with total card fraud losses falling from £439.4 million in 2005 to £428.0 million in 2006, a decrease of nearly £80 million over the past two years. This fall has been driven by a 13% decrease in UK domestic fraud and the combined reduction of more than £45 million in fraud from mail non-receipt and from lost and stolen cards. These and other changes in fraud losses between 2004 and 2006 are illustrated in Table 1.

The introduction of Chip and PIN made it more difficult for fraudsters to commit card fraud in the UK, with losses at UK retailers falling by £146.7 million over the period 2004-06 *despite increasing card transaction turnover by value and by volume.* However, criminals are still able to copy the magnetic stripe data. They use these data to create counterfeit magnetic stripe cards that can be used in countries that have not upgraded to Chip and PIN. This has caused an increase in fraud abroad losses over the last 12 months, after a slower than expected initial displacement, and one might anticipate that this trend will continue. After all, it is cheaper and quicker to travel by rail from London to Paris than it is from London to

Table 1: Credit and Debit Card Fraud Losses on UK-Issued Cards Split by Fraud Type

Fraud Type	2006 (+/-change on 2005)	2005	2004
Counterfeit (skimmed/ cloned) card fraud	£99.6m (+3%)	£96.8m	£129.7m
Fraud on stolen or lost cards	£68.4m (−23%)	£89.0m	£114.5m
Card-not-present fraud (phone/internet/mail)	£212.6m (+16%)	£183.2m	£150.8m
Mail non-receipt	£15.4m (−62%)	£40.0m	£72.9m
Card ID theft	£31.9m (+5%)	£30.5m	£36.9m
TOTAL	£428.0m (−3%)	£439.4m	£504.8m
Contained within this total:			
UK retailer (face-to-face transactions)	£72.1m (−47%)	£135.9m	£218.8m
Cash machine fraud	£61.9m (−6%)	£65.8m	£74.6m
Domestic/International split of total figure:			
Fraud within the UK	£309.8m (−13%)	£356.6m	£412.3m
Fraud abroad	£118.2m (+43%)	£82.8m	£92.5m

Source: APACS.

Liverpool, so cross-border fraud has to be seen in the context of effort for criminals: sophisticated language skills are not needed for purchases on payment cards overseas! Over the same time period, card-not-present fraud losses increased by 16%, and in 2006 accounted for just under 50% of all card fraud losses. To put total fraud losses further into context, however, UK card issuer losses as a percentage of plastic card turnover equated to 0.095% in 2006 – significantly less than the 0.141% figure in 2004.[7]

A number of measures are currently in place to tackle card-not-present and online fraud, such as an automated cardholder address verification and card security code system, and *MasterCard SecureCode* (www.master

card.com/uk/securecode) and *Verified by Visa* (www.visaeurope.com/veri-fied). Cardholders simply need to register a private password with their card company for use when shopping online at participating retailers. The banking industry has worked on the next generation of fraud prevention solutions to help tackle fraud in non face-to-face transactions (i.e., e-banking and Internet and telephone shopping).

APACS liaised with banks, card schemes, retailers, trade associations and systems vendors on the implementation of a trial of one such solution that builds upon Chip and PIN technology and will enhance the online protection already offered by systems such as *MasterCard SecureCode* and *Verified by Visa*. In the spring of 2007, Barclays became the first major card issuer and bank to issue free card readers for one-time only passwords for online banking transactions like bill payments and transfers to third parties. Many others are likewise issuing card readers into which a card has to be inserted or USB "dongles" that are personalized and do not require the insertion of a card. Only one major UK bank in mid-2007 does not currently intend to do this, on the grounds that its e-fraud problems are under control and it is not cost-effective to spend funds on such measures (though if adaptation by fraudsters occurs, the impact of other banks introducing controls may increase its vulnerability, showing that cost effectiveness of controls is a shifting dynamic).

In the period 2002-6, the UK payments card industry:

- Invested £1.1 billion in the rollout of Chip and PIN.

- Established the Dedicated Cheque and Plastic Crime Unit (DCPCU), the special police unit that specifically tackles plastic card and check fraud, with a funding commitment of £3 million per year by the bank-ing industry.

- Promoted retailer take-up of the Industry Hot Card File (IHCF), an electronic database that enables retailers to check whether a card is being used fraudulently. Over 335,000 cases of attempted fraud were prevented by this system in 2006. The system has been used at mo-torway tollbooths in France to combat the use of stolen UK cards to pay for road tolls (and, when identified and cards retrieved, to prevent further use).

In 2006, APACS extended its fraud reporting beyond cards to include other payment industry fraud losses, including fraudulent encashments (the fraudulent withdrawal of cash over a branch counter) and losses due to forged instructions (fraudulent requests to transfer funds from a bank account). These non-card related payment fraud losses in total amounted to £72.2 million in 2006. Contained within this figure are online banking fraud losses (the majority of which were forged requests), which totalled £33.5 million in 2006. This is an increase of 44% year-on-year and has been driven by an increase in identified phishing incidents,[8] which rose from 1,713 in 2005 to 14,156 in 2006. As is the way in media reportage, the rise in e-losses became the focus of attention. Check fraud also continues to fall, due to the industry's continuing success in identifying most fraudulent checks as they go through the clearing process, coupled with better public awareness of the issue and declining check use. As shown in Table 2, losses fell from £40.3 million during 2005 to £30.6 million in 2006, a decrease of 24%.

CIFAS AND UK CROSS-INDUSTRY DATA-SHARING

CIFAS (formerly the Credit Industry Avoidance System) data illustrate the rise in some forms of fraud, though the like-for-like changes are difficult to unpack because of increases in CIFAS membership.[9] Table 3 shows a summary of the statistics and the number of fraud cases filed by CIFAS members between 2006 and 2007, disaggregated by the type of fraud identified.[10] In 2007, detected application fraud (in which fraudsters tell lies on application forms in order to obtain credit, insurance or other products) increased by 20%, identity frauds fell 3%, and facility takeover cases filed rose by over a third (although the base rate of cases filed is smaller). For reasons that are currently obscure, there has been a swing away from previous-address fraud towards current-address fraud.[11]

There is ongoing activity to reduce fraud losses. As losses of identity documents increased due to corporate data protection security breaches,

Table 2: Other UK Fraud Losses Split by Fraud Type

Fraud Type	2006 (+/-change on 2005)	2005	2004
Check fraud	£30.6m (−24%)	£40.3m	£46.2m
Online banking fraud	£33.5m (+44%)	£23.2m	£12.2m

Source: APACS.

Table 3: CIFAS UK Cases by Type, 2006 and 2007

Fraud type	Jan to Dec 2006	Jan to Dec 2007	% Change
Identity Fraud – Granted	28,340	32,175	13.53%
Identity Fraud – Not Granted	52,037	45,418	–12.72%
Identity Fraud – TOTAL	**80,377**	**77,593**	–3.46%
Application Fraud – Granted	8,805	14,515	64.85%
Application Fraud – Not Granted	55,055	62,355	13.26%
Application Fraud – TOTAL	**63,860**	**76,870**	**20.37%**
False Insurance Claim	395	390	–1.27%
Facility Takeover Fraud	4,665	6,272	34.45%
Asset Conversion	440	478	8.64%
Misuse of Facility	21,751	23,400	7.58%
Victims of Impersonation	67,406	65,043	–3.51%

CIFAS responded by introducing a Bulk Protective Registration Service in 2007 that allows companies to co-ordinate and submit in bulk to the CIFAS database the details of all those customers who require protection. Before doing so, in accordance with the Data Protection Act, a company must inform its customers of the data breach and that their personal data is being processed by CIFAS to complete the Protective Registration. Until 2007, this service was available only to individuals. It allows those who are at risk of identity theft to have a special CIFAS "flag" placed on their credit reference agency file. When, for example, an application for credit or insurance is received by a CIFAS member (such as a bank or building society), the Member is then alerted by the "flag" to make additional verification checks to ascertain that the applicant is genuine, and not a fraudster trying to commit identity theft. If they do not take these additional verification measures, or if the fraudster eludes the checks, then fraud remains possible.

FROM CARD FRAUD TO "IDENTITY FRAUD"

In the 21st century, "identity fraud" (or "identity theft," though it is mostly duplication or "borrowing" rather than a pure zero-sum game), has become a particularly popular theme in the electronic and print media; in spite of guarantees by many card issuers to consumers against suffering losses from fraud when making Internet purchases, it appears to evoke significant levels of fear. Awareness campaigns are popular with vendors not just of physical security such as shredders but also of paid-for services (including those from the banking industry), and there are annual "Identity Theft" awareness weeks in the UK "badged" by the Home Office but largely paid for by the industry, with local media events around the country.

Paid-for services in the UK and US include "fraud alerts" with credit reference agencies such as Experian and Equifax that may tell you if someone has applied for credit in your name (but not, apparently, in the US if they have used your social security number with a different name); or indeed programs that hide one's IP address when going on-line.[12] Fear of crime and judgments about its probability and consequences might plausibly be viewed from the perspective of different participants, who may have very different levels of knowledge and experience, and may directly (as with bank financial crime directors) or indirectly (as contributors to Trusted Third Party industry-wide data bodies like CIFAS in the UK or to the liquidators/trustees of pyramid/securities fraud schemes) share their experiences to pool data as closed user groups (see Levi and Pithouse, forthcoming). In some cases, like CIFAS and the Insurance Fraud Bureau in the UK, this fraud data sharing has a primarily preventative function, managing business risks collectively; in others, it serves less of a future crime-proofing function and more as a venue for communicating victim experiences and obtaining a share, however modest, in the payout from the assets of the defaulting firm or individual.

There are also differences in offender and victim perspectives. As Semmens puts it:

> The perpetrator of this kind of crime is simply using information, raw data, in the course of his/her criminal activities. By assuming control of information which does not "belong" to him/her, s/he takes advantage of the pure instrumental value of the information. In contrast, the victim who loses control of the information attaches both instrumental and intrinsic value to that information and this impacts on the victim's identity. In short, the criminal act is simply the 'theft of identifying information" but the victim suffers "theft of identity." (2003:ch. 7)

The Home Office Identity Theft website also offers the following definitions (http://www.identity-theft.org.uk/definition.html):

- Identity fraud and identity theft are often used very loosely to describe any situation in which personal details are misappropriated for gain.

- Identity crime is a generic term for identity theft, creating a false identity or committing identity fraud.

- False identity is: (a) a fictitious (i.e., invented) identity; or (b) an existing (i.e., genuine) identity that has been altered to create a fictitious identity.

- Identity theft occurs when sufficient information about an identity is obtained to facilitate identity fraud, irrespective of whether, in the case of an individual, the victim is alive or dead.

- Identity fraud occurs when a false identity or someone else's identity details are used to support unlawful activity, or when someone avoids obligation/liability by falsely claiming that he/she was the victim of identity fraud. Examples of identity fraud include using a false identity or someone else's identity details (e.g. name, address, previous address, date of birth and etc.) for commercial, economic or monetary gain; or obtaining goods or information; or obtaining access to facilities or services (such as opening a bank account, applying for benefit or obtaining a loan/credit card).

While there is some reason for aggregating the creation and circulation of fictitious or copied/misattributed personal data – for example in what might be a category of "application fraud" and/or "corporate website fraud" – there is an unfortunate tendency to include within "identity fraud" any conduct that involves an individual pretending to be someone he/she is not (e.g., using a stolen credit card, social security benefit book, or a World Cup/FA Cup Final ticket).[13] Furthermore, there is an even worse elision between "identity fraud" and "identity theft," with the latter being applied to any illicit access to personal data, whether or not it is used for any criminal purpose (including fraud). Thus every time a financial institution or a government or municipal department leaves any personal data exposed (in the garbage or online), this tends to be described as "identity theft."

Although the examples given by the Home Office Identity Fraud Steering Committee relate to fraud, in theory they could include unlawful activities that are not fraud in the normal sense. For example, they could include: a) fraud that gives people the right to reside in the UK, but following which they do not defraud tax or social security or commit other offences, or b) identity fraud that facilitates terrorism, but involves no other financial deceptions. It is arguable that in the UK, such conduct could be brought within the "causing loss" provisions of the Fraud Act

2006, but if there were evidence of this, other more serious offences might be charged. From a preventative viewpoint, it seems unlikely that the change in criminal law will have an immediate impact unless it makes data sharing easier or endangers intermediaries who may have some legitimate reputation or assets to lose from being drawn into the criminal net.

Jones and Levi (2000) distinguished between cases where elements of another individual's identity are "borrowed" and those in which an entire identity is "developed," which could more properly be described as "theft." In cases of application fraud, where the criminal uses another individual's information to set up a credit agreement or loan, there may be (depending on crime control efforts) a need for a portfolio of personal data. Typically, these offences will require the criminal to acquire a combination of attributed and biographical data: proof of name and address (three year history), a sound credit history, date of birth, proof of income and employment details. Therefore, for most applications – buttressed also by UK Money Laundering Regulations – it will be necessary for the criminal to produce documentary evidence in the form of a passport/birth certificate, utility bills, bank statements and pay slips in order to establish his/her identity. These documents will then need to be acquired from the victim (through loss or theft) or acquired via "address impersonation" (Jones and Levi, 2000; see also the CIFAS discussion earlier).

A fraudster living in rented property may intercept the post of either the current property owner (the landlord) and/or other current occupants of the house (where it is a shared tenancy or multiple occupancy household of a type commonly found among students). Second, the fraudster might target previous occupants of the property, usually by taking receipt of post that has been sent to the old address by mistake. Finally, despite controls at the Royal Mail, it may be possible for the fraudster to adopt the name and current address of another individual and then register his/her own address as if that individual has moved house. Once the fraudster has managed to collect a series of documents (utility bills, bank/payment card statements or pre-approved card/loan applications) s/he can go on to apply for loans, or where necessary, acquire further documentary evidence (see Jones and Levi, 2000).

Identity theft in its stronger sense is most easily achieved where the victim is deceased, especially where the victim died in infancy and has not already built a portfolio of biographical data (Jones and Levi, 2000). In such a case, the fraudster may find the details of a deceased child in a graveyard, selecting one with a date of birth close to his/her own (Cabinet

Office, 2002). From this point, it is relatively easy to obtain a birth certificate, which then becomes an important "breeder document." The difficulties of closing this gap – highlighted in Frederick Forsyth's popular 1970s novel and film *The Day of the Jackal* – generated much alarm but little action until 2006 because the costs of change fall upon the separate agency, while the benefits fall elsewhere; this is yet another example of the problems of uneven incentives in government-wide or public-private cost-benefit analysis. In this case, the externalities are dumped by a public sector agency onto other public sectors, private sectors, and individuals who incur fraud and terrorism risks.

However, there has been a flurry of activity since 2006, stimulated not just by fraud but also by terrorism controls over false identities and the desire to minimise contamination of a national ID register. Thus, the Identity and Passport Agency (IPS) has instituted a programme of controls over passport applicants including: Interviews; Biographical Footprint Checks; Facial Recognition; Biometric enrolment/Fingerprints; a Fraud Key Performance Indicator to reduce its level of undetected application fraud below 0.15% of passport applications; and measures to monitor counter-signatories and serial passport losers.

Since the legislative changes in 2006, all applications are now checked against an infant death database, which contains 750,000 infant death records and is available to other agencies for cross-checking. All passports are now sent by secure delivery and IPS has seven Fraud and Intelligence Units. Checks are being introduced against adult death data and Border and Immigration databases. Applicants will be photographed as they arrive for interview at the regional centres being established, and these will be matched against existing ones as well as (presumably) acting as a deterrent. In short, quite apart from any alarms to individuals over the risks of identity fraud to induce them to take greater care (and to pay for hardware or software protection), there is substantial industry change to mitigate risks, under the watchful eye of a reinvigorated (but still understaffed for litigation) Information Commissioner's Office.

SOME COMPARISONS WITH THE US

How does the reform of identity theft and card fraud differ in the US? The card market is more fractured in the US, since the same financial institutions seldom act as both card issuers and merchant acquirers (reimbursing merchants for a fee for the transactions they undertake). Despite some mega-mergers in the US banking system, this has made it harder to co-ordinate action against fraud. As is the case also in many other European countries, card fraud data are unavailable for the US.

As for identity fraud, on the basis of a detailed telephone survey of 5,000 adult victims[14] (out of an initial sample of 25,000 adult Americans), Javelin Strategy & Research (2007:5) asserts:

> In the last year, 8.4 million Americans became the victims of identity fraud, half a million fewer victims than the year before. The total fraud amount dropped 12%, from $55.7 billion to $49.3 billion . . . In the last year, the average victim of an existing account fraud paid $587 out-of-pocket in consumer costs. If the thief opened a new account in the victim's name, the average consumer had to pay $617.

It is helpful to distinguish between advice to business and advice to individuals, the latter predominating in the "responsibilisation" process. It should be stressed that traditionally, much more public information is available about American "personal identifiers" such as social security numbers than is the case in Britain, so the effort involved for criminals in the UK is greater. American consumers are advised to take the following steps: to establish credit report fraud alerts, to close tampered accounts, and to file a police report and a complaint with the Federal Trade Commission (FTC) itself.[15] After that the individual is conditioned to actively canvass credit reference agencies, creditors, debt collectors and the police to extricate actual and potential fraudulent accounts from their credit record – all the time being informed of their rights, duties and obligations. This exercise of "active citizenship" requires as much conscientiousness as does health monitoring, and there are various "check up guides" available.

The Fair and Accurate Credit Transactions Act of 2003 was motivated in large part by the perceived need of the federal state to improve identity theft prevention and resolution (Linnhoff and Langenderfer, 2004), inter alia enshrining for the first time the right of consumers to a free annual credit report from each of the three national credit referencing agencies. More so than the UK, the US has available – from companies like the credit score modelling firm, Fair Isaac, and the three national credit reference agencies – online access to credit scores, for a fee, so that consumers can manage their creditworthiness. For a mere $4.95 per month, Fair Isaac's "Identity Theft Security Deluxe" (http://www.myfico.com/Products/IDF/Description.aspx):

- tracks your TransUnion credit report and more than 400 other data sources for signs of identity theft;

- provides identity theft resolution help should you become a victim; and,
- Includes identity theft insurance coverage up to $25,000.

The general thrust of paid-for service in the US is aimed at potential victim self-awareness and self-help, assisted by the firms (rather like motoring organizations after car breakdowns) to minimize harm before the individual's credit-worthiness is destroyed; this is particularly important because one cannot effectively be a citizen unless one has access to credit (unless you are very rich). Identity theft, as in the UK, has spawned some profitable insurance protection products for individuals, as well as advice for businesses (e.g., http://www.ftc.gov/bcp/edu/pubs/business/idtheft/bus59.shtm).

CONCLUSIONS

In conclusion, it is apparent that the struggle against card and card-related fraud has been a difficult one, with global network brands such as Visa and MasterCard, card issuers, merchant acquirers, retailers and credit reference agencies acting in a sometimes conflictual, sometimes harmonious way alongside consumers and law enforcement agencies, and those who aim to defraud them. As Chip and PIN become more universal in Europe and the Far East, US-issued cards become relatively softer targets and it seems plausible that whether inside the US or overseas, those cards will be hit harder, changing the cost-benefit ratio for prevention measures. On the other hand, it may be harder to generate an organisational forum for prevention within the US; while within Europe, the European Payments Council now plays a greater role, as part of the move towards the Single European Payment Area (SEPA), mandated by the European Commission as part of the European single market. Largely due to controls established to deal with card present fraud, the main arena of struggle now appears to be in the card-not-present environment. The more we give out personal identifiers for a variety of transactions, on-line and off-line, the greater the probability that at some stage, a recipient of that information will pass it on to fraudsters and/or other motivated offenders. The criminal use that can be made with that depends on how far biometric data as well as pattern analysis can be used nationally and transnationally to keep fraud within manageable bounds.

Address correspondence to: Michael Levi, Cardiff University, School of Social Sciences, Glamorgan Building, Cardiff CF10 3WT, Wales, UK; e-mail: Levi@Cardiff.ac.uk

NOTES

1. See Levi et al. (2003) for a more general discussion of business attitudes towards crime control.

2. Apart from problems of retailer recognition of photos – a significant issue affecting preventative power – a national rollout would have required massive numbers of passport-photo type machines, which then might not have alternative uses, forcing them to be written down in value more rapidly for accounting purposes. This does not mean that for any one card issuer, it is pointless to put photos on cards. If only a few cards have photos on them, thieves/fences may discard them since there are many other cards that do not present problems requiring some degree of impersonation, e.g. cross-age, cross-gender, and cross-race. Customers also may like them and even feel more secure, rationally or not.

3. A smart card, chip card, or integrated circuit card (ICC), is a pocket-sized card with embedded integrated circuits which can process information. It can receive input which is processed – via the ICC applications – and delivered as an output.

4. In 1967, a year after Barclaycard started up as the first European credit card, 85 French banks started issuing the Carte Bleu, which had no international links. Initially, the system was conceived to process invoices automatically at merchants via an optical reading device, for direct debiting to their customers' accounts. However this generated many errors and high costs, and the Carte Bleu initiative improved only when a network of ATMs was added. In 1973, Carte Bleu became internationally connected via an agreement with Bank Americard.

5. The designers sought to design in fraud prevention. The most effective way to do it is to have a special private key in each card and a chip powerful enough to use it to produce a certificate that shows a terminal that it is genuine. The terminal holds a *public key* corresponding to the private one, which it uses to check the authenticity of the certificate. If the terminal is dismantled, discovering the public key is not enough to counterfeit a card: the fraudster must discover the

private key which remains safe within the card. The EMV designers call this method "Dynamic Data Authentication." However, there is a less effective but cheaper method called "Static Data Authentication" where a single key is shared between each card and the bank that issued it. This key is used to authenticate the transaction, and produce the "transaction certificate." The terminal does not know this key. The card can prove to the terminal that it is genuine, but only if that terminal is online, that is, connected to the card issuer or acquirer via a phone line. Offline machines, however, have no way of telling if the card is genuine on the spot. They can record the response the card gives during authorisation, and pass it on to the financial institution when they next reconnect, but there is nothing they can do immediately. The fraudster does not need to know this PIN because it is the card's job to verify the PIN and respond with a yes/no answer to the terminal. Seeing as the card is a counterfeit, the fraudster can program it to say "yes" no matter what PIN is entered. Banks understandably do not publish what sort of authentication they have funded but in the longer term, DDA may be necessary. For a sceptical critique, see http://www.chipandspin.co.uk/problems. html#smartcard, though one should add that the ability to crack communications does not mean that compromises can be industrialized, which is what fraudsters would need.

6. This is also a generic problem with the bureaucratic process of rolling out pilot results nationwide, since to the extent that observed improvements are affected by charisma, the latter is not replicable universally, at least pending major genetic changes!

7. Profitability figures – which might be a driver for cost-benefit assessment and for investment in fraud prevention – are unavailable.

8. "Phishing" is the attempt to obtain sensitive access/identity information, such as usernames, passwords and payment card details, by masquerading as a trustworthy entity in an electronic communication. It is typically carried out by email (or telephone contact), and directs users to enter details at a website pretending to be a legitimate one.

9. I am grateful to fraud prevention service CIFAS for these data and discussions about them. As of 2008, CIFAS has 270 member organizations spread across banking, credit cards, asset finance, retail credit, mail order, insurance, investment management, telecommunications, factoring and share dealing. Members share information about identified frauds in the fight to prevent further fraud. Its members state

that they saved almost £1 billion in 2007 as a result of shared filings on suspected persons, which saved them from lending to persons to whom they would otherwise have given credit. The data would properly need to be split to hold membership and range of activities constant in order for trends to be consistent over time.

10. *Identity fraud* cases include cases of false identity, identity theft, account takeover and other impersonation situations. *Application fraud/ False insurance claim* relates to applications (e.g. for finance) or claims (e.g. for insurance) that include material falsehood or false supporting documentation where the name has not been identified as false. *Facility takeover* occurs where a person (the "Facility Hijacker") unlawfully obtains access to details of an existing account holder or policy holder or an account or policy of a genuine customer or policy holder (the "victim of takeover") and fraudulently operates the account or policy for his own benefit or the benefit of another unauthorized person. *Asset conversion* relates to the sale of assets subject to a credit agreement where the lender retained ownership of the asset. *Misuse of facility* is where an account, policy or other facility is obtained for fraudulent purposes or the fraudulent misuse of a facility.

11. *Current-address fraud* is a type of identity fraud where the victim lives at the "current address" given on the fraudulent application. The perpetrator of the fraud is often also resident at the same property as the victim. In such cases, the fraudster applies for, and uses, products in the name of the victim whose property they share. The fraudster will generally have access to, or can intercept, the victim's post, for example where individuals are resident at a property that has a communal mailbox with shared access. Other contributory factors to current address fraud can include the abuse of Companies House data, data breaches, fraudulent mail redirections and bin raiding. *Previous-address fraud* is where the fraudster misappropriates the identity of another person and falsely claims that the victim has recently changed address. Due to the short period of time at the "new" address, any Credit Reference Agency checks are performed primarily against the "previous" address where the victim is, in reality, still resident. In such circumstances, the fraudster will usually apply in the name of the victim for new products and will undertake facility takeover fraud from the "new" address.

12. One such product, Zone Alarm's Anonymous Surfing, claims that it "protects you and your family from online identity theft by keeping

your IP address (and your identity) private. It also protects you from visiting phishing, pharming, or spyware sites by displaying a warning notification of the hidden dangers ahead" (www.zonealarm.com). Many other products such as Internet Explorer 7 now offer phishing filters as defaults in response both to consumer anxieties and objective risks, though objective risks by themselves do not create a market.

13. The Home Office's (2006) updated cost estimates include £395 million for money laundering, despite the statement alongside that the proportion of money laundering properly attributable to identity fraud was unknown, adding: "The figure from the original study has been included for illustrative purposes to help estimate any comparative changes to the overall cost of identity fraud since 2002" (ibid:3). In other words, although the data have never been defensible, their exclusion might lead to a lower total ID fraud figure, which might be embarrassing. To a lesser extent, this also applies to revenue ID fraud data.

14. Identity fraud is defined by Javelin Strategy & Research as follows: "the unauthorized use of some portion of another's personal information to achieve illicit financial gain. Identity fraud can occur without identity theft. For example, it can occur with relatives who are given access to personal information or by the use of randomly generated payment card numbers" (2007:15).

15. "ID theft: when bad things happen to your good name," Federal Trade Commission (http://www.popcenter.org/Problems/Supplemental_Material/identity_theft/BadThings_2000.pdf); "Identity theft: what to do if it happens to you," Fact Sheet 17a, Privacy Rights Clearinghouse (http://www.privacyrights.org/fs/fs17a.htm); "Financial identity theft: the beginning steps," Fact Sheet 100, Identity Theft Resource Center, October 2005; "Financial identity theft: more complex cases," Fact Sheet 100A, Identity Theft Resource Center, October 2005 (http://www.idtheftcenter.org).

REFERENCES

Cabinet Office (2002). *Identity fraud: A study*. London, UK Her Majesty's Stationery Office. Available at: http://www.homeoffice.gov.uk/docs/id_fraud-report.pdf

Home Office (2006). *Identity fraud update*. London, UK. Available at: http://www.identity-theft.org.uk/ID%20fraud%20table.pdf

Jones, G. and M. Levi (2000). "The value of identity and the need for authenticity." Research Paper, *Turning the Corner: Crime 2020*. Available at: http://www.foresight.gov.uk/Previous_Rounds/Foresight_1999__2002/Crime_Prevention/Reports/Turning%20the%20Corner/essay5.htm

Javelin Strategy & Research (2007). *2007 identity fraud survey report – consumer version: How consumers can protect themselves*. Available at: http://www.javelinstrategy.com/

Levi, M. (1992). "Preventing credit card fraud." *Security Journal* 3(3):147-153.

Levi, M., P. Bissell and T. Richardson (1991). *The prevention of cheque and credit card fraud*. Crime Prevention Unit Paper 26. London, UK; Home Office.

Levi, M. and J. Handley (1998). *The prevention of plastic and cheque fraud revisited*. Home Office Research Study 182. London, UK; Home Office.

Levi, M., J. Morgan and J. Burrows (2003). "Enhancing Business Crime Reduction: UK Directors" Responsibilities to Review the Impact of Crime on Business." *Security Journal* 16(4):7-28.

Levi, M. and A. Pithouse (forthcoming). *White-collar crime and its victims*. Oxford, UK: Clarendon Press.

Linnhoff, S., and J. Langenderfer (2004). "Identity theft legislation: The Fair and Accurate Credit Transactions Act of 2003 and the road not taken." *Journal of Consumer Affairs* 38(2):204–16.

Semmens, N. (2003). *Fear of plastic fraud*. Unpublished Ph.D. thesis, University of Sheffield, UK.

Webb, B. (1996). "Preventing plastic card fraud in the UK." *Security Journal* 7(1):23-25.

PREVENTING IDENTITY-RELATED CRIME: THE CHALLENGES OF IDENTIFICATION

by

Russell G. Smith

Principal Criminologist
Australian Institute of Criminology

Abstract: *This chapter provides a framework for assessing the competing factors that need to be addressed when determining how to minimise risks associated with crimes involving the misuse of documents and other evidence used to establish identity. Three approaches are possible: the traditional approach, which relies on the production of documents of varying degrees of security; using biometric technologies such as fingerprinting or facial scanning; and using identity cards such as those that make use of computer chips secured with a Personal Identification Number. Ten groups of factors are identified against which each system can be assessed, and a framework for quantitative analysis is provided. Selecting an appropriate and effective system, or combination of systems, requires the evaluation of a considerable and ever-increasing body of technical evidence relating to the performance of systems, in addition to an examination of a range of social, legal, and practical considerations to do with privacy, data security, user acceptance, and cost. Compelling evidence of performance should not, however, overwhelm these non-technological considerations. It is concluded that the* *adoption of any given solution must be driven by an objective assessment of evidence relating to all of these factors – not solely those governing technical performance measures.*

INTRODUCTION

Identifying people with certainty is both a time-consuming and costly exercise for public and private sector organisations. Each year, government agencies need to identify millions of new residents, millions of voting enrolment forms need to be processed by electoral offices, revenue agencies need to register new taxpayers and businesses, social security agencies need to identify new applicants for benefits and those to whom benefits should be paid, and foreign affairs agencies need to identify applicants for passports and visas. On each occasion, evidence of identity is required.

In addition, millions of people every day log-on to computer networks for work, to withdraw cash from Automated Teller (Banking) Machines, or to use the Internet for recreation or business. Most do so using a password. There are also millions of occasions each year upon which individuals need to be identified for access to buildings, travel purposes, collection of highway tolls, and use of retail customer cards in shops.

Failure to have effective means of identification creates many opportunities for criminal activity, which include obtaining finance dishonestly, opening bank accounts in false names, money laundering, motor vehicle re-birthing, credit card skimming, obtaining social security benefits, obtaining security guard licences and shooters' licences, avoiding driving demerit points, producing certificates for immigrants, and terrorist-related activities.

The incidence of identity-related crime has increased considerably since the advent of computers and the Internet owing to the ability of digital technologies to facilitate the fabrication and alteration of documents used to establish identity, and to enable personal information to be located with ease from electronic databases. In the United States, a representative survey of 5,000 adults found that 4% of the adult population had been victims of identity fraud in 2005 (Javelin Strategy & Research, 2006). In Canada, a national survey conducted in mid-March 2005 with 1,000 Canadians (aged 18 years and older) found that 20% had been victims of identity theft – an increase of 5% on the corresponding figure from the 2003 survey (Canadian Competition Bureau Report, 2005). In Australia, identity-related fraud was estimated to cost (A)$1.1 billion in 2002 (Cuganesan and Lacey, 2003). Clearly, the opportunities for criminal misuse of identity are being exploited on a wide scale by criminals across the world.

This chapter examines the ways in which government agencies have responded to the problem of identity fraud in recent times. It provides a framework for evaluating three principal approaches to identifying people for government and business purposes: the conventional approach, which relies on the submission and verification of evidence of identity documents; the use of biometric systems, such as fingerprinting or facial scanning; and the use of identity cards, especially the most advanced kinds which have information secured using computer chips activated by a Personal Identification Number (Chip/PIN).

IDENTIFICATION SYSTEMS

Document-Based Systems

Conventional document-based systems, which currently operate throughout the developed world, rely on people submitting documents for inspection by the staff of government agencies or financial institutions. Under some systems designed to identify people who open bank accounts, each document is assigned a value depending upon its level of security. Primary documents, for example, including certificates of citizenship, passports, and birth certificates, are assigned the highest number of points (in Australia, for example, 70 points each). Secondary documents, including drivers' licences (40 points), public employee or student ID cards (40 points), credit cards (25 points), health care cards (25 points), and council property rates notices (25 points), are assigned lower numbers of points. There is a range of other documents that can be relied on to verify one's name and address, each carrying different numbers of points. At present, in Australia, for example, 100 points of documentation are required in order to open an account with a financial institution as well as for establishing one's identity for the most secure forms of electronic communications with government. Unfortunately, documents are relatively easy to counterfeit or to alter, making it possible for criminals to make use of another person's identity without their knowledge, or to create an entirely fictitious identity which can then be used for the commission of a range of criminal activities.

Biometrics

In recent years, the technologies of biometrics have developed greatly as a means for identifying people. Biometrics has been defined by the United Kingdom Biometrics Working Group (2002:4) as " . . . the automated means of recognising a living person through the measurement of distinguishing physiological or behavioural traits." In other words, biometric systems are based on who people are, rather than what people carry with them such as a card, or what they know, such as a password. Whether by fingerprint, voiceprint, iris or facial pattern, or a number of other characteristics, it is possible to measure individuals' personal attributes to help to identify them. In Australia, for example, on 24 October 2005, a biometrically-enabled passport was first made available in which the personal information currently recorded on the passport is kept on a computer chip embedded in the centre pages of the document. Already many thousands of e-passports have been issued, with trials being conducted involving airline staff and some others enabling them to use facial recognition technology in conjunction with the e-Passport to proceed through customs controls at airports (Nash, 2005).

Identity Cards

A third approach is to issue people with identity cards that are a simple form of token-based system in which individuals can produce or disclose something that they possess. It is now possible for plastic identity cards to contain a computer chip that can hold personal data in a more secure way than occurs with ordinary magnetic stripe cards, which are vulnerable to compromise through "skimming." In order to provide a further layer of security, computer chip cards can be activated through the use of a PIN, or even a biometric authentication system.

In recent times with ever-present concerns over terrorism, a number of countries have decided to issue compulsory identity cards, some of which include a biometric identifier. The Special Administrative Region (SAR) of Hong Kong, for example, has developed multi-use ID "smartcards" that contain basic biometric information such as thumb prints and a photograph, and are capable of multiple functions including use as drivers' licences and as library cards (Benitez, 2002). A pilot program for a biometric ID card has also been implemented in Britain, in relation to asylum seekers (McAuliffe, 2002). In Britain, financial institutions have also issued Chip/PIN cards which must be used by all users after 13 February 2006 when making card transactions.

IDENTIFICATION PROCESSES: ENROLMENT AND MATCHING

Each of these three systems involves the use of two processes: enrolment and matching. In the enrolment phase, an individual's identifying information (such as documentary evidence, or a fingerprint in the case of biometrics) is acquired for the first time. Biometric images are converted into a "template," against which subsequent comparisons are made. In the case of document-based systems and identity cards, the individual's identity is checked against previously registered data held on databases of other issuing agencies or on a card, which may or may not be secured by a PIN or other security measures.

At present, when individuals seek to carry out transactions with government agencies or banks, they simply produce their card, state their name or provide a signature. This can then be verified against previously held data. In the matching phase of a biometric system, an individual's biometric characteristic is captured again. This "live template" is compared against previously enrolled data, seeking a match. In the matching phase of a card-based system, the cardholder simply presents the card for matching against a variety of characteristics such as signature, photograph, or PIN (in the case of chip cards). Matching cards of course requires the cardholder to physically hand over the card or at least present it for scanning in the case of contact-less card systems such as those used in Hong Kong's transport system.

CHOOSING THE BEST APPROACH

The ways in which these three systems can be evaluated differ depending upon the particular type of technology and security measures used, as well as the purpose for which the system is being used – whether for identification or for surveillance/"watch list" checking. No single test has been developed that can accurately measure all issues across different systems in a uniform way. Because of this multiplicity of ways in which systems can be evaluated, it is difficult to determine which is the "best" approach, because some systems will perform well on one measure but will be outperformed on others. The choice of which system to deploy, if any, will depend on the particular needs and priorities of the organisation, including the location and purpose of the system, and the number and nature of the people who will be using it.

Policy makers are faced with a wide range of considerations to be assessed when deciding whether or not to implement any particular solution to deal with identity-related crime. On the one hand, they must evaluate a considerable and ever-increasing body of technical evidence relating to the performance of technologies, while on the other hand a range of social, legal, and practical considerations need to be addressed including privacy, data security, user acceptance, and cost. There are ten key groups of factors that need to be assessed when making a decision to go down one path or another. Table 1 sets out a simple calculus to compare these various considerations. For each factor, it is possible to rate its effectiveness, which represents a balance between its benefits (in terms of the extent to which the system will overcome the problems sought to be addressed in minimising identity fraud risks) and its harms (in terms of any negative consequences associated with its introduction). Each system can then be compared in terms of its mean benefit / harm value determined using the following formula:

$$v = \frac{\Sigma(w(b) \times s(b))}{\Sigma(w(h) \times s(h))}$$

where:
v = value
b = benefit
h = harm
w = design importance weighting (1-5)
s = practical significance score (1-5)

To calculate the mean benefit/harm value for each identification system, it is possible to assign a design weighting from 1 to 5 according to each factor's importance in terms of the system's benefit (e.g., 5 = greatest benefit) or harm (e.g., 5 = greatest harm). For example, in relation to the risk of false enrolment when opening back accounts using a document-based system, the way in which evidence of identity is used is of critical importance in assessing the effectiveness of the system in preventing identity fraud. Hence, it would receive a design importance weighting in terms of benefit of 5, and a design importance weighting in terms of harm also of 5. This is because opening a bank account using false documentary evidence creates a high degree of harm for both banks and customers,

Table 1: Evaluative Calculus for Competing Identification Systems

Factor	Documentary systems (bank accounts)						Biometrics (facial scanning)						Identity cards (chip/PIN)					
	Benefit			Harm			Benefit			Harm			Benefit			Harm		
	W	S	W.S	W	S	W.S	W	S	W.S	W	S	W.S	W	S	W.S	W	S	W.S
Enrolment																		
1. Failure to enrol																		
2. False enrolment																		
Matching																		
3. Failure to acquire																		
4. False match																		
5. False non-match																		
6. False accept																		
7. False reject																		
8. Equal error rate																		
Efficiency																		
9. Enrolment speed																		
10. Matching speed																		
11. Data overload																		
Data Security																		
12. Portable medium																		
13. Database																		
Spoofing																		
14. Artificial identities																		
15. Relay attacks																		
16. Database attacks																		
Privacy																		
17. No consent																		
18. Function creep																		
19. Unauthorised data matching																		
User Acceptance																		
20. Links to police																		
21. Links to criminals																		
22. Health and safety																		

Factor	Documentary systems (bank accounts)						Biometrics (facial scanning)						Identity cards (chip/PIN)					
	Benefit			Harm			Benefit			Harm			Benefit			Harm		
	w	s	w.s	w	s	w.s	w	s	w.s	w	s	w.s	w	s	w.s	w	s	w.s
Rectification																		
23. Inability to rectify																		
24. Cost of																		
25. Time to carry out																		
Costs																		
26. Infrastructure																		
27. Implementation																		
28. Recurrent																		
Displacement																		
29. Spatial																		
30. Temporal																		
31. Target																		
32. Tactical																		
33. Offence																		
34. Perpetrator																		
Column Total																		
Column Mean																		
Mean Benefit / Harm Value																		

w = weight (1-5); s = score (1-5); w.s = weight x score (1 - 25)

while having adequate systems in place to guard against the acceptance of false evidence of identity represents a considerable benefit in terms of reducing identity fraud. The design importance weighting, therefore, is an objective measure of the balance between risks and benefits for the specific way in which the system is *designed*.

It is then helpful to assign a score from 1 to 5 to determine the practical significance of the factor, again in terms of both its benefit and its harms. Practical significance means simply the extent to which the system succeeds in achieving its objectives (for benefits), or the extent to which harms actually arise. In the case of false enrolment when opening bank accounts using a document-based system, the benefit that is actually achieved when using current legislation that requires certain types of documents to be produced as evidence of identity would, arguably, in Australia (for example) be scored as 3 in terms of its benefits in avoiding identity fraud, and as 4 in terms of the associated harms. The practical significance score, therefore, provides an assessment of how well the system *operates in practice* in any given localised circumstances.

It is then possible to multiply the design importance weighting values by the practical significance score values for each factor to obtain an overall assessment of the impact of that factor. In the example of using document-based systems to prevent false enrolment with banks, the total benefit score would be 15 and the total harm score 20. Once such scores have been calculated for all the factors for each system – which will vary from 1 (least effective) to 25 (most effective) – it would be possible to make comparisons between systems.

It is important when undertaking any such assessment of competing systems that specific rather than general approaches be compared. Clearly, it would be inappropriate to compare "biometric systems" as a whole, in view of the widely differing performance of specific technologies. For example, comparisons could be made between a document-based system used to open bank accounts; facial recognition biometric systems such as that being implemented by the Australian Customs Service; and the use of a computer chip identity card with PIN authentication, such as that being used in the SAR of Hong Kong. Confining the discussion in this way would, hopefully, permit greater comparability to be achieved across the various approaches, without the introduction of other confounding factors. Ideally, assessments of this nature would draw on the results of empirically-based research, and/or be undertaken by informed stakeholders in the provision of the systems in question. The primary arguments applicable to each group of factors are discussed below.

EVALUATIVE CRITERIA

Enrolment

Each system requires users to identify themselves upon enrolment. At the outset, it is important to bear in mind that the ways in which identity is established under a document-based system will still be required for biometric and card-based systems, although the electronic capture of a biometric can be accomplished in seconds as opposed to the somewhat lengthy process of issuing and activating a card. Appropriate evidence of identity is required under each system, which may include background checks with referees or interviews. The integrity of any system is only as good as the quality of the enrolment data provided. In the case of biometrics, a real danger arises if a person can successfully bind their biometric data to a stolen identity, because this will allow them to continue using the stolen or fabricated identity for a variety of fraudulent purposes, with little risk of detection. Two primary measures of performance on enrolment are the failure-to-enrol rate, which measures the proportion of users who for some reason cannot enrol in a particular system; and the false-enrolment rate, which measures the extent to which users are able to enrol using a false identity.

Matching

The performance of matching processes can be measured in a variety of ways. Matching of identity cards raises few difficulties as cards are simply issued to eligible people, who can present them for matching when required. Chip/PIN cards, however, involve certain performance issues that arise in common with biometric systems. The following measures can be used to assess matching performance:

- *Failure-to-acquire rate* – This measures the proportion of cases where a user seeks to provide a biometric to match against their previously enrolled template, but the system cannot acquire an image of sufficient quality.

- *False-match rate* – This measures the probability that a sample will be falsely declared to match the template of another person.

- *False-non-match rate* – This measures the probability that a sample will be falsely declared not to match the template of the user who provided the sample.

- *False-accept rate* – This measures the proportion of cases in which an impostor is falsely accepted by a biometric system.

- *False-reject rate* – This measures the proportion of cases in which a genuine user is falsely rejected by a biometric system.

- *Equal-error rate* – This is usually the point at which the false reject and false accept rates are equivalent. In some cases, it can also refer to the point at which the false match and false non-match rates are equivalent.

It should be noted that while these measures are widely used in the biometrics industry, their use is not always consistent. Evaluations are also often carried out within the industry promoting the technology in question, thus casting doubts on the objectivity of some reports. This makes it vital for policy makers to inspect any evaluation report closely before accepting its results.

Efficiency

An important consideration for all identification systems is their ability to be used by agencies to deal with extremely large numbers of individuals quickly. It is possible to assess speed in a number of ways. These include looking at the time taken to enrol a person, to acquire their characteristics, to verify information provided, or to conduct the matching process. Biometric systems vary considerably in relation to their processing speeds, although they are invariably quicker than the manual processing of individuals in a document-based system or when using plastic cards. Where systems fail for some reason, however, considerable time may be taken to rectify the problem. The problem of data overload also needs to be considered prior to implementing an electronic system on a national or international scale.

Data Security

Data in both biometric and card-based systems may be stored in either of two ways. Each offers its own challenges and risks. When cards are employed to verify individuals, biometrics systems seek to compare individuals' body samples – such as their facial images – directly with a template recorded on the card or other portable medium. If this is the case, then defeating that medium's security features may allow replacement or alteration of the template, unbeknown to the system administrators. For facial recognition, this might be as straightforward as photo substitution or as complex as cracking strongly encrypted data held in a Chip/PIN card system.

If on the other hand, the comparison were to a template held on a central database, that database would represent a high-profile target for criminals. Securing that information represents a major challenge, although public key encryption systems can be effective in ensuring data security. These entail the use of encryption in which data are scrambled or encoded in an attempt to guarantee that only the intended recipient can read the information. Trusted third parties then vet and vouch for the identities of users when they transmit the encrypted information. Security risks of central databases also arise from individuals within organisations who may seek to gain access to and alter information inappropriately. In recent times, outsiders and insiders alike have defeated various large-scale information databases. In May 2005, for example, a U.S. processor of payment card data – CardSystems Inc. – had its database breached and the information (including magnetic stripe data and cardholder names) relating to over 40 million credit card accounts was stolen (Krim and Barbaro, 2005). To anticipate the points of susceptibility to interference is the essential challenge of implementing both biometric applications and card-based approaches on a wide scale.

With established databases, such as those held by revenue agencies or registries of births, deaths and marriages, there is also an on-going need to cleanse the data to ensure that the information recorded about individuals is correct. Some changes that occur may be legitimate, such as changes of name on marriage or through formal change of name procedures. Others, however, are dishonest.

Spoofing (Counterfeiting)

All three systems are susceptible to spoofing – or compromise through counterfeiting or deceiving the security measures in question. In the case of card-based systems, circumvention entails an individual acquiring the required card by stealing or purchasing a legitimately manufactured card, or forging a copy. The ease with which cards can be counterfeited will depend on the nature of the card, and any security features (such as holographic images) that have been incorporated. Although the use of such security features may make it more difficult to defraud card-based systems, with advances in computer technology it is usually possible for a determined identity thief to bypass even the most secure systems and counterfeit cards containing the appropriate security features. Even if documents cannot be successfully counterfeited, it may still be possible to buy or to steal them.

In the case of chip cards, counterfeiting would require that the chip's encryption be defeated, which is beyond the ability and resources of most criminals. A simpler approach to defeating a chip card activated with a PIN, is to ascertain the PIN. This may be learnt directly from the user or the user may be tricked into revealing it through "social engineering." Alternatively, it may be guessed or "cracked" through the use of computer technology, or may be obtained through practices such as "shoulder-surfing" (where an individual watches a person entering their PIN into a machine) or "dumpster-diving" (where an individual searches through a person's rubbish for relevant information).

In the case of biometric systems, there are three main ways in which a system can be attacked (Thalheim et al., 2002). The first involves the creation of an artificial biometric by putting artificially created data into the regular sensor technology of the system. For example, a photograph could be used to deceive a facial recognition system. For this approach to work, it is necessary for the impostor to obtain a copy of the biometric that they wish to use such as by taking a photograph of the person to be imitated. The problem of displaying this to the sensor in public then also needs to be addressed.

The second method, known as relay attacks, involves the use of artificially created data. Instead of obtaining the relevant data by copying the biometric to be used, this method involves capturing the relevant data as they are input into the sensor, through use of a device such as a sniffer program, perhaps attached to a computer's USB port. The data captured can then be replayed, to deceive the system. A researcher at the Australian National University in 2002, for example, demonstrated how a template resembling that electronically stored in the device could be used to circumvent fingerprint verifiers (Baker, 2002).

Finally, there are database attacks that seek to compromise the databases in which the data are stored. This will usually need to be done by someone who has administrator rights over the database, although it could be done through hacking. One way such an attack could take place is where an individual who works on the development of the system forges user data that are reactivated at a later date to their advantage.

In developing technologies, however, manufacturers have attempted to create countermeasures – the most common of which is known as "liveness" testing, which ensures that the biometric characteristic being measured belongs to a live person. For example, facial recognition systems may require evidence of eye movements or temperature sensors. Such systems have dual advantages in that they can help to prevent spoofing, as well as potentially preventing some forms of crime displacement (see below).

There is little research that has measured the ability of systems to repel concerted attacks. Facial recognition systems, for example, have yet to be tested against people seriously motivated to evade detection through prosthetic and cosmetic adjustments to their facial shape and size. Indeed, partial facial transplants have recently been performed which could affect template matching. In one study conducted by three German researchers, efforts were made to spoof a number of different biometric systems (Thalheim et al., 2002). While some caused them slight difficulties, they managed to compromise each biometric system investigated with a little persistence.

Privacy

Recording personal information and its retention in large databases raise various privacy concerns. While some have claimed that biometrics can be a privacy-enhancing technology (Biometrics Institute, 2002), there is a general perception that the use of such technologies is likely to invade privacy. Similarly, there are concerns that the use of identity cards may infringe privacy more than enhance it. The widespread implementation of identity cards or biometrics systems faces vocal opposition from privacy advocates, who raise the grave consequences of information being misused, such as occurred during the Nazi regime in the Second World War. One writer refers to " . . . the singular ease with which population registration systems have been mobilized for genocidal purposes" (Seltzer, 1998:544).

Some of the main privacy concerns that affect both biometric and card-based systems include fears that information will be gathered without permission or knowledge, or without explicitly defining the purpose for which it is required. That information may be used for a variety of purposes other than those for which it was originally acquired ("function creep"); shared without explicit permission; or used to track people across multiple databases to amalgamate information for the purpose of surveillance or social control (U.S. General Accounting Office, 2002).

Any use of such systems needs to comply with privacy principles and privacy legislation (Crompton, 2002). In the case of biometrics and Chip/PIN identity cards, additional measures may be needed to mandate the use of specified levels of encryption for the capture, storage and transmission of data, to limit database matching except under close scrutiny by independent observers, to prevent the reconstruction or retention of the original biometric sample from encrypted biometric information, and to prevent comparisons with reproductions of biometric information not obtained directly from individuals. Some of these aspects may require amendments to privacy legislation.

User Acceptance

Past experience has shown that the efficiency and accuracy, particularly of biometric systems, can be reduced if those required to use the system are not willing to accept the technology. Some people may find the process of providing personal information in public distasteful. This was one reason given for the reluctance of retailers to make use of a cheque fraud prevention initiative that required customers to leave their fingerprint on cheques before retailers would accept them (see Pidco, 1996). Similarly, users may associate fingerprints with policing or criminality and feel reluctant to use fingerprinting systems. Still others may believe that iris or retina scanning systems may harm their eyes (despite clear evidence to the contrary). Accordingly, the need arises to educate users about the reasons why the system has been introduced and how it might benefit them. User concerns relating to privacy and the security of data storage, as well as the safety of using some devices (especially eye-based biometrics), would also need to be addressed.

Rectification

Another problem associated with biometrics more than identity cards arises from the fact that once a system has been compromised, it may be difficult to rectify the problem. While a new card or PIN can always be issued, new facial images cannot. Even if the enrolment process remains error-free, a biometric is effectively a "PIN you can never change" – and compromised once, is compromised for all time (Biometrics Institute, 2002).

Cost

There are a wide range of costs involved in the implementation and use of each system, although both biometric and Chip/PIN systems have extensive initial implementation costs. It is especially important to consider recurrent costs, which can often outweigh the costs of infrastructure and initial implementation. In evaluating systems, it is important to examine these different cost considerations separately, and to conduct evaluations of recurrent costs once implemented.

Displacement

Finally, the use of any highly secure identification systems as a crime reduction strategy carries with it the risk that displacement may occur. One academic described the problem of displacement of crime as follows: "Fear of displacement is often based on the assumption that offenders are like predatory animals (they will do what ever it takes to commit crimes just as a rat will do whatever it takes to steal food from the cupboard)" (Eck, 1998:602). If it is assumed that potential offenders act on the basis of some rational calculation in which they balance up the likely risks and benefits to be derived from a potential course of conduct, then as some types of crime are seen to become too difficult to commit, other easier targets may be considered. Theorists have identified six ways in which criminal activity might be displaced following the introduction of crime prevention measures: displacement of crime to other locations (spatial); displacement of crime to other times or occasions (temporal); displacement to softer targets (target); displacement through different modus operandi (tactical); displacement to other types of crime (offence); and displacement to other perpetrators (perpetrator).

The use of biometrics or chip/PIN cards could result in offenders obtaining access to computers through bribery or coercion of IT personnel, or forcing users under threat of violence to disclose their PIN or to permit the offender to have access by presenting their biometric under duress. We have already seen the occurrence of this with duress being used by offenders against users at Automated Teller (Banking) Machines to compel them to withdraw cash. Failure to comply has even resulted in users being killed in some countries (Smith et al., 2003).

CONCLUSIONS

In deciding whether or not to implement different types of personal identification systems, policy makers need to ensure that the new technology does not make matters worse – either with respect to the specific crime problem to be addressed, or by creating new risks through the infringement of privacy or displacement to other forms of more serious crime. Careful thought also needs to be given to what technologies cannot do. Of greatest importance is the fact that they cannot validate identity upon initial enrolment. If checks are not in place to validate the evidence of identity produced upon enrolment, then the subsequent use of a biometric authentication system may make identity-related crime easier to perpetrate, and more difficult to detect.

Another important need is to balance the evidence that exists in support of, and against, any given system in relation to each of the various considerations outlined above. Policy makers should avoid the temptation solely to focus on the seemingly convincing evidence of technical performance provided by the industry concerned. Technical performance is only one criterion, and even this can be measured in a wide range of ways. Instead, evidence needs to be sought out and scrutinized concerning the range of other legal, social, and ethical considerations governing the use of any given system. Unfortunately, it is these aspects that have yet to be fully researched.

Address correspondence to: Russell Smith, c/o Australian Institute of Criminology, GPO Box 2944, Canberra, ACT, 2601, Australia; e-mail: Russell.Smith@aic.gov.au

Acknowledgments: I am grateful to former colleagues at the Australian Institute of Criminology, Jamie Walvisch, Dr Yuka Sakurai and Stuart Candy who helped with background research for an earlier, shorter version of this chapter, which was published in the Australian Institute of Criminology's series *Trends and Issues in Crime and Criminal Justice* (No. 324, 2006) as "Identification Systems: A Risk Assessment Framework." The views expressed are not necessarily those of the Australian Government.

REFERENCES

Baker, L. (2002). "Rule of thumb: Don't rely on new security systems." *ANU Reporter* 33(9):1.

Benitez, M.A. (2002, February 27). "ID card contract awarded." *South China Morning Post* (Hong Kong), p. 2.

Biometrics Institute (2002). *The impact of biometrics on privacy: An interview with Dr. Roger Clarke.* Available at: http://www.biometricsinstitute.org/bi/interviews.htm

Canadian Competition Bureau (2005). *Findings from the 2005 Fraud Awareness Tracking Study.* Ottawa, Canada: author.

Crompton, M. (2002, March 20). *Biometrics and privacy: The end of the world as we know it or the white knight of privacy?* Paper presented at the Biometrics-Security and Authentication Biometrics Institute Conference, Sydney.

Cuganesan, S. and D. Lacey (2003). *Identity fraud in Australia: An evaluation of its nature, cost and extent.* Sydney: Securities Industry Research Centre of Asia-Pacific.

Eck, J (1998). "Preventing Crime at Places", In L.W Sherman, D. Gottfredson, D. Mackenzie, J. Eck, P. Reuter and S. Bushway (Eds.), *What Works, What*

Doesn't, What's Promising (pp. 573-619). Washington, D.C. U.S. National Institute of Justice.

Javelin Strategy & Research (2006). *Identity Fraud Survey Report.* Pleasanton, CA.

Krim, J. and M. Barbaro (2005, June 18). "40 Million Credit Card Numbers Hacked." *Washington Post*, p. A01. Available at: http://www.washingtonpost.com/wpdyn/content/article/2005/06/17/AR2005061701031_2.html

McAuliffe, W. (2002, February 5). "Asylum seekers get first UK biometric ID cards." *ZDNet Australia.* Available at: http://www.zdnet.com.au/newstech/security/story/0,2000024985,20263301,00.htm

Nash, B. (2005, November 1). *Utilising the latest in biometrics technology to enhance your forensic capability.* Paper presented at the Institute for International Research conference Combating Identity Fraud, Sydney.

Pidco, G.W. (1996). "Check print: A discussion of a crime prevention initiative that failed." *Security Journal* 7(1):37-40.

Seltzer, W. (1998). "Population statistics, the Holocaust, and the Nuremberg Trials." *Population and Development Review* 24(3):511-552.

Smith R.G., N. Wolanin and G. Worthington (2003). "E-crime solutions and crime displacement." *Trends and Issues in Crime and Criminal Justice* #243. Available at: http://www.aic.gov.au/publications/tandi/tandi243.html

Thalheim, L., J. Krissler and P-M. Ziegler (2002, May 11). "Body check: Biometric access protection devices and their programs put to the test." *c't Magazine.* Available at: http://www.heise.de/ct/english/02/11/114/

United Kingdom Biometrics Working Group (2002). *Use of biometrics for identification: Advice on product selection.* Available at: http://www.cesg.gov.uk/site/ast/biometrics/media/Biometrics%20Advice.pdf

U.S. General Accounting Office (2002). *Technology assessment: Using biometrics for border security.* GAO-03-174. Washington, D.C. Available at: http://www.gao.gov/new.items/d03174.pdf

PREVENTING IDENTITY THEFT THROUGH INFORMATION TECHNOLOGY

by

Sara Berg
School of Criminal Justice
University at Albany

Abstract: *Identity theft is one of the fastest growing high-tech crimes in the United States, due in part to the easy availability of personal information. Although this information can be obtained both physically and through the use of computers or the Internet, information technology (IT) strategies could also make it harder to do. This paper applies eight selected techniques of situational crime prevention to show how IT can be used in identity theft prevention. Computer security methods harden potential targets and extend guardianship. Physical and digital controls decrease offenders' access to facilities. Validation of personal identity can deflect offenders. Firewalls will conceal computing targets. Information markets can be disrupted. Login banners act as a means to post instructions to offenders and warn them of penalties for unauthorized access. Finally, employee training can alert consciousness about victimization. Although situational crime prevention is generally carried out at the organizational level, IT-based approaches can also be applied to an individual level of protection. However, a concluding argument is made that, given the ubiquitous nature of personal information, even IT protection may not matter in the end.*

Crime Prevention Studies, volume 23 (2008), pp. 151–167.

INTRODUCTION

Identity theft is one of the fastest growing high-tech crimes in the United States today. Also known as identity fraud, these two interchangeable labels refer to the commission of several types of fraud in the United States and other nations, although naming conventions vary in crime statutes and in practice throughout the world. Identity theft is committed by obtaining unique personal information and then using it to impersonate one or more victims, in one or more locations across time – spanning hours to years. Various methods are used in order to gain access to information for identity theft purposes, among which a key piece of data is a person's Social Security Number (SSN). This crime causes both financial and emotional harm to its victims, making this computer-based offense just as dangerous to consumers as traditional personal and property crimes committed "offline."

In order to understand how identity theft could become so prevalent in the United States (see Synovate, 2003; Javelin Strategy & Research, 2005, 2006, 2007), it is important to recognize two major advances. First, we have electronic banking and credit cards, which have made modern life convenient. Second, we have SSNs, which have become an easy way to keep track of an individual. The theft of an individual's "identity" is not a new phenomenon. This form of fraud, where someone socially misrepresents him or herself as another, has always existed. However, the misuse of credit card numbers and SSNs – an individual's key pieces of personal identification – has resulted in the growth of the financial fraud that is today called identity theft.

METHODS OF COMMITTING IDENTITY THEFT

Although some victims are not aware of how an offender obtained their personal identification information, there are a number of different methods that enable the theft to occur (see National Center for Victims of Crime, 2001; U.S. Senate, 2000). Stealing the victim's purse or wallet may provide access to a great deal of data, including name, address, date of birth, driver's license, phone number, credit cards, and most importantly, Social Security Number. If a SSN cannot be immediately found, it can be purchased through online information brokers when details such as name and birth date are given. These information brokers, alternatively, can sell SSNs as well, getting the numbers from credit report headers.

Using a technique known as "dumpster diving," offenders search the trashcans of individuals or businesses for documents that might contain

SSNs or other data. Related to this is mail theft, where documents, such as pre-approved credit card applications, are stolen directly from a mailbox. A change-of-address form can similarly be used to divert a victim's mail to the offender, which potentially provides the offender with the victim's personal information. Within a company, dishonest employees with access to sensitive data can also obtain SSNs and other records.

Personal and credit information can further be taken from unsecured online (Internet-based) shopping sites. Using "pretexting," a method for obtaining personal information under false pretenses (Federal Trade Commission, 2006), an offender could pose as a telemarketer or a financial representative to lure victims into disclosing key pieces of information. So-called "phishing" schemes are used by offenders who seek to direct consumers to input their account information into a fake web site designed to look like the site for a legitimate business such as eBay, PayPal, or financial institutions; these scams are often sent via e-mail, with the e-mail also appearing to come from a legitimate business. Finally, it could be a relative, friend, or someone else with a personal relationship with the victim who may divulge and/or use their information to perpetrate identity theft.

Clearly, even though identity theft has been identified as a high-tech crime, not all of the methods used in order to acquire personal information are information technology (IT) based. This is especially true of techniques such as purse or wallet theft, dumpster diving, or mail theft. However, the interconnectedness of financial databases has resulted in an integration of both physical and IT means to perpetrate acts of identity theft. Information technology comes into play once an offender uses the personal information, such as SSN or credit card number, which is physically taken from the victim. Additionally, the incorporation of IT has it made possible to commit identity theft on a large scale, thus changing the dynamics of both offending and victimization. Offenders may work together in organized groups, may never physically meet in person, and may never come into physical contact with their victims. As one article puts it, identity theft is the "neoteric [modern] crime of the information technology era" (Saunders and Zucker, 1999:184).

SITUATIONAL CRIME PREVENTION

Situational crime prevention (SCP) is a strategy designed to reduce opportunities for crime through the application of five main principles: (1)

increase the effort required for offenders to reach their target; (2) increase the risks for offenders if they commit crime; (3) reduce the rewards of a successful crime; (4) reduce the provocations that may entice offenders into making greater efforts to commit crime; and (5) remove the excuses for committing crime. These approaches have been expanded into a list of 25 techniques, each addressing specific aspects of these main ideas (Center for Problem-Oriented Policing, 2006). Although not all 25 SCP techniques can be applied to high-tech crimes, a number of them can easily be adapted to fit technology-enabled offenses. This chapter selects eight techniques to demonstrate how IT can be used to prevent identity theft (see also chapters by Newman and Willison in this volume for other applications of SCP to the problem of identity theft).

Increase the Effort: Target Harden and Increase the Risks: Extend Guardianship

A variety of security techniques can be used to harden computer system targets and extend guardianship to them. Target hardening is a way to increase the effort needed by an offender; it may still be possible to access the target, but it will generally take more time and resources. Similarly, extending guardianship will increase the offender's risk of detection and/ or apprehension and make it more likely that s/he will be caught prior to committing the intended criminal activity. Information technology measures to implement these techniques include anti-virus software, firewalls, patching, data encryption, and "strong" passwords (see below).

Anti-virus software is designed to detect and eliminate malware – malicious coding that takes the form of viruses, worms, or "Trojans"[1] – from a computer system. Malware can be installed in a number of ways, such as opening an e-mail attachment, visiting a web page, or executing a file. Once a system is infected, malware could, unbeknownst to the user, delete or corrupt files, slow system performance, or install an application such as a keystroke logger. The latter becomes the biggest identity theft threat; programs like keystroke loggers could record a user's password, such as one associated with an online bank, and then send it to the offender. In order for anti-virus software to be effective, its virus definitions must be regularly updated to reflect current threats. One limitation, however, is that updated definitions are only released as fast as the company making the software can provide a means to detect and neutralize new malware. This can cause a delay in time between the release of malware and the release of updated virus definitions.

Data encryption is a way of encoding data so that it is not readable without special information or knowledge. A cipher (algorithm) is used to transform otherwise plain text data into a coded format that is unreadable until it is deciphered, and a key is required on the user's end to "unlock" the original data. In recent months, there have been dozens of incidents where laptops containing sensitive information were lost or stolen from government or private organizations. If the data on these machines were encrypted, it would not matter if it fell into the hands of a criminal because the information would be worthless to them unless they had the decryption key. While it is possible to break certain forms of encryption, thus making it possible to view the data, this requires a certain amount of knowledge about ciphers as well as computing power. Unless the motivated offender who finds a quick opportunity in stealing an unattended laptop is also a skilled hacker, or someone who has solicited the services of a cryptographer, he or she will be unable to use the information it contains.

All machines should be updated with the most recent operating system and software patches to prevent vulnerabilities from being exploited. A patch is a piece of data, released by a vendor, which is applied to that vendor's existing code/application on a system. Although patches may improve functionality, more often they are released to close a security vulnerability that has been discovered. For example, Microsoft releases security patches on a monthly basis so that users of the Windows operating system (OS) will be protected against "exploits" found after the OS was initially released.[2] An offender with knowledge of an exploit can gain access to an unprotected system, potentially enabling him or her to view sensitive files such as those containing personal information. While "zero-day" exploits are possible, allowing an attacker to take advantage of the vulnerability on the day it is made publicly known, it is more likely that an offender will use a well-established exploit for which a patch is available but not yet applied.

Employee workstations and company mainframes should be protected by strong passwords that are difficult for outsiders to guess or hack. A strong password is one with eight or more alphanumeric characters, including at least one number and one symbol and a mix of upper and lower-case letters, which cannot be found in a dictionary. So-called cracker programs exist that enable an offender to run through lists of dictionary words and attempt to use them as account passwords. If the password is alphanumeric and contains symbols, it becomes harder to use brute force for guessing purposes. Although it is possible to write programs that would guess strong passwords, it would take much longer to obtain a password this way, as opposed to a dictionary program that could guess the password quickly. Effective password management through IT would require a user to select a strong password at its initial creation, in addition to forcing a password change after a certain time period has passed (e.g., every 90 or 180 days) and not allowing multiple passwords to be used on the same system or network.

Increase the Effort: Control Access to Facilities

By controlling access to facilities, an offender's effort must increase if s/he is to gain entry; this is another strategy to strengthen capable guardianship. Here, facilities can be either physical (e.g., buildings or computer server rooms) or digital (e.g., a computer system is the "facility" for IT services). All computer systems should have physical protection in place, in addition to IT-based logical protection, that restricts system access among both inside employees and outside individuals. Information security is too often viewed as being solely concerned with the security of digital assets, but in practice, even digital assets have a tangible form (e.g., server hardware, electronic media, or printouts of data). Hardware should be secured behind locked doors with the key, combination code, and/or ID card limited to only essential individuals. Policies that prohibit employee/visitor possession or use of electronic media – such as USB drives, floppy disks, iPods, or cellular phones – are intended to prevent sensitive documents from being taken in and out of a facility. Data printed on hard copies should be secured in much the same manner as hardware or shredded before disposal so that an offender could not obtain it from the trash.

The buildings themselves that house computer systems or other sensitive information should also have controlled access. This can be implemented through previously mentioned measures such as a key, combination code, and/or ID card. In addition, computer-supported surveillance systems should be secured to prevent possible breaches. An offender who can disable the surveillance system could then gain entry to the building and acquire sensitive information through a physical interior search.

Information technology can be used to provide computer-based controls for systems, as well as controls for software. Internally-used software applications should be designed in a manner that limits data access solely to those employees who need it for their work. Not everyone will need permission to view or change all of the organization's information. Permission should instead be delineated by responsibility, with individuals able to access only what they require to carry out their job function. Implementation measures include password management (different passwords for different data), firewall usage (access to certain parts of a network depends on job function), or "roles," such as those found in Oracle's database application. Each default role includes a set of permissions, which can be altered depending on an organization's needs and an employee's function. A database administrator working directly in Oracle tables, for example, will have a role providing more extensive access than an end user who only needs to view three pieces of data through a Microsoft Access interface.

Increase the Effort: Deflect Offenders

Organizations should better validate personal identity prior to authorizing financial transactions, such as approving a loan or credit card payment, in order to deflect offenders and make it harder for them to fraudulently use personal information. The United States is a land of instant credit, which is one factor in the increased growth of identity theft. Merchants are often unwilling to alter their processes to help prevent identity theft if they feel that this will create difficulties in consumers being able to obtain credit (Sullivan, 2004). It has been said that " . . . [f]inancial services providers (FSPs) might be encouraging identity theft through aggressive marketing practices" including "[t]he mass mailings of pre-approved applications" (Wheatman et al., 2002:para. 2). According to the Gryphon Foundation (2001), " . . . [b]ecause of competitive pressures, many creditors will not take time to confirm the identity of the person who accepts the pre-approved offer. For businesses, the economic incentive is to write off losses due to credit card fraud as a cost of doing business" (para. 30). This stance has created friction between victims, who complain that the commercial industry has not done enough to prevent victimization, and merchants, who do not want to lose potential customers if credit authorization takes too long.

Clearly, there must be a compromise for offering better identity verification that will not take the "instant" out of "instant credit." As computing resources improve and connections become faster, merchants could obtain high-speed links to a verification database server. Since it is not merely enough to check that a Social Security Number is valid in order to prevent identity theft, the assorted pieces of data that comprise an individual's financial identity must also be validated to ensure that they match together correctly. Is the address given on a credit card or loan application the correct address on file? Is the date of birth correct? Does the mother's maiden name match? This computerized checking is important because, although various technical systems can catch fraudulent activity more effectively than humans alone, IT is not infallible. To that end, human workers must also do their part to verify identity, providing a dual-layer system of man and machine working together. There is a negative side of central information repositories, though; they could be the target of government inquiries, either permissible or law-violating, or the target of hackers and other offenders. This would also be the case if a national ID card were created as a means for better validation, since it would become a new object for offenders to acquire.

While credit card numbers are certainly powerful, the large number of incidents that stem from fraudulent SSN use illustrate an even greater power. The Social Security Number is a key piece of information for an offender, as it is an identifier within various databases in the United States. Even when other data are faulty, a valid SSN can open many doors. On any application, the name, address, date of birth, and other fields may all be incorrect, but as long as the SSN is right it is extremely easy for the offender to get credit, loans, or other lines of finance. Again, validation systems need to be employed here to detect potential misuses of personal information and ensure that an individual cannot gain access to existing or new accounts, or commit other fraudulent acts, with only a single piece of victim data.

Validation processes must be undertaken regardless of whether the application or transaction is made online or offline (e.g., in a store or at a bank). The address and other information given in an application should be checked to see if they match what is on file in an individual's credit report. As noted above, it is not enough to check to see whether the SSN is correct. Signature analysis programs could also be used to verify that the signature being given is the correct one for the named individual. A database of signatures could be stored for a company, and then every time a person does business with them, their signature would be checked against the database.

Reduce the Rewards: Conceal Targets

Offender rewards will be reduced if their targets are concealed, and this can easily be done through the use of IT. Social Security numbers are a prime target for offenders due to their ubiquity and their necessity for many financial transactions (e.g., obtaining loans, filling out credit card applications, and opening utility accounts). Although the original intent for the SSN was that it would be used as a unique identifier solely within the U.S. Social Security Administration, today it is used in a variety of organizations. Ideally, the practice of using an SSN as an individual's main identifier should be eliminated, or at least scaled back – if this is even possible. Its easy availability in everyday life has helped set the conditions for its misuse. Therefore, reducing its widespread usage would result in a reduced risk of identity theft victimization.

To do so, the SSN would need to be replaced with some other unique identifier, and any forms of identification that previously listed the SSN would need to be reprinted with the new ID number. While many businesses have not taken this action, claiming that it is prohibitively expensive, the costs of these modifications have been said to be negligible compared to the cost of organizational preparation for the "Y2K" (1999 into 2000) calendar-year change (Computer Professionals for Social Responsibility, 2002). In practice, though, " . . . the costs of identity theft and loss of privacy may outweigh the institutional costs of modified database practices" (ibid:para. 10). It would be cheaper to mask SSNs in existing databases or to create a different identifier in new databases than to reimburse the financial losses or repair harm to the reputations of institutions that become victimized. That said, even if a new unique identifier were used, it would most likely have the same problems as an SSN; the target of identity theft offenders would simply shift. Similarly, there is also no way of knowing if this database modification will produce problems in the future, just as programmers lacked the foresight to consider the impact of the proliferation of computers in the late 20th century – which resulted in "Y2K."

Firewalls can also be used as a means of concealing computer-based targets. The term "firewall" originally referred to brick walls built between apartment buildings to prevent a fire from spreading between them (Oppliger, 1997). Today's firewall is a logical device that isolates a computer or network from the Internet as a whole through the implementation of Access Control Lists (ACLs). These ACLs must be properly configured to allow only permitted network traffic in and out of an intranet (private internal network), as well as to protect what is behind a certain portion of a network so that those outside the network cannot see or gain access to what is within it. Personal computers (PCs) generally include firewall software as a default option, but firewalls are even more important for the public and private sectors of business. Sensitive corporate and government data – including SSNs, credit card numbers, health care records, and employment information – could be prime targets for offenders looking to commit identity theft. Storing this data behind a firewall will protect it from an outside criminal threat, although it would not necessarily prevent an insider from stealing the information.

Reduce the Rewards: Disrupt Markets

As with tangible goods, an underground ("black") market exists for data that can be used to commit identity theft. If this market can be disrupted, it would make it more difficult for offenders. The proliferation of Internet-based information brokers has made it extremely easy to obtain personal information, often for a low price. Individuals can purchase data such as Social Security Numbers, addresses, phone numbers, and dates of birth that are then used in fraudulent financial transactions. Although it is certainly possible to obtain many of these details from public records, consolidated information databases provide them in an easily accessible and centralized location. Eliminating these sites would then require offenders to manually search in a number of different places to find the information needed to commit identity theft.

In addition to online information brokers, markets exist on private networks such as Internet Relay Chat (IRC). Users of these free servers can log on and make contact with other users on an international level. "IRC bots"[3] are one means for users to provide Peer-to-Peer (P2P) filesharing. If used for this purpose, these bots often facilitate the unrestricted sharing of *warez* files (pirated software) and child pornography, but they could also be used to distribute stolen personal information. Some networks may have policies that disallow running bots on any server, while others may leave the decision to the server administrator; either way, if forbidden bots are discovered, the user can be removed temporarily or banned permanently from the server/network. There are also web sites and bulletin boards where personal information is traded between users. A crackdown on these sites, by having their service providers and hosting companies shut them down once discovered, would also help to eliminate identity trafficking. If illegal information dissemination is occurring on an otherwise legitimate site, the offending user can be removed and his or her access blocked in this case as well.

Yet who or what organization/government agency will be responsible for monitoring? IRC server administrators or operators can look for IRC bots and remove them, as noted above, but it would be more difficult to examine content on the World Wide Web. According to Netcraft (http://news.netcraft.com), a United Kingdom company that has been keeping Internet statistics since 1995, there were over 150 million web sites in existence as of January 2008. Any monitoring would thus need to be automated, perhaps through the use of "web spiders" – programs that traverse web pages for content. Spiders, however, may only index a fraction of a site's content, especially if they are designed for breadth and not depth (Introna and Nissenbaum, 2000). If web site operators use a large company to host their pages, spiders might not pick up any illegal content on the page. The spider may also not be able to access posts on a bulletin board advertising illegal activity.

Remove Excuses: Post Instructions

One way to "remove excuses" for offenders is to post instructions that their intended course of action is criminal. A primary way to inform individuals about illegal system intrusions is to provide a login banner either prior to or after logging in. This statement makes it clear as to who is allowed to use the system and warns of the penalties for unauthorized access. It may also be a legal requirement to advertise that system access will be monitored and tracked, regardless of whether the access is permitted or not (Malik, 2002). Similarly, acceptable use policies detail what types of computing activities are allowed and what types are forbidden. As many cyber offenders are insiders, companies can use these policies as a means to detail what employees can or cannot do when using resources at work. Users may also be held to Accessible Use Policy standards for accessing resources belonging to their Internet Service Provider or another organization.

Nevertheless, it is difficult to say how effective this measure would be. Instructions exist in other forms, such as the Federal Bureau of Investigation's anti-piracy warning statement at the beginning of movies on DVD, but these DVDs are still copied and sold. An individual may not read the warning; and even if s/he does read it, they may not care to follow it. As per the rational choice perspective, they could weigh the costs and benefits of committing an act and decide that the benefits are greater, and accountability may matter here. Individuals who do not follow the posted instruction, regardless of what form it takes, should be held responsible for their actions – be the result a fine, jail time, getting fired, losing some sort of privilege, or some other type of sanction.

Remove Excuses: Alert Conscience

More training for commercial and financial employees will alert their conscience and actively increase awareness about how to prevent victimization. Following a training session, employees should be able to recognize situations that have the potential of leading to identity theft victimization and know what steps they can take in order to stop them. This training can be implemented using IT by offering computer-based instructional modules combining text, audio, and video. Instead of static training videos, interactive methods might better engage an individual and provide a means of testing whether the content is being learned. Using the concept of Intelligent Computer-Based Instruction (ICBI), scenarios could be designed and given to employees to test them. If the employee fails to recognize a potential identity theft incident or identify the preventive measures that should be taken, the training can then be targeted to address specific weaknesses. The use of a game as an immersive instruction tool is also touted as generating meaningful learning, as its players are able to apply what is learned in the real world (Foreman, 2003). Combining these two techniques could overcome the direct learning weaknesses generally seen in gaming situations since games are not necessarily conducive to supporting educational aims (Siemer and Angelides, 1995:1376). An intelligent simulation would adapt to the individual's educational needs, assess learning achievement, and provide immediate feedback to users about their progress (ibid).

Situational Crime Prevention for the Individual

The techniques of situational crime prevention are often applied to organizations, but when it comes to computer-based identity theft incidents, organizations are not the only victims. *Individuals* can also implement many situational crime prevention measures, thereby taking responsibility for protecting themselves against victimization. Computer security measures are vital for user PCs, as most store some kind of personal information that identity theft offenders could use if access were obtained. Users need to run anti-virus software, have a properly configured firewall, patch their systems, and use strong passwords. Computers – especially portable laptops – should not be left unattended in unsecured areas, and doors and windows should be locked and fastened within a secured area.

However, the best individual measure for preventing identity theft is education, and training mechanisms could be also developed to test individuals on the concepts of general identity theft prevention. While there would not be the same sort of mandate for individuals to engage in this training as would exist for corporate employees, there are some situations in which one could be in effect. Schools, especially colleges and universities, can incorporate prevention education training as part of other classes, in stand-alone seminars, or during new student (e.g., freshman or transfer) orientations. Training modules could be part of software installations; instead of merely checking a box to show that they have read the licensing agreement, the user would also have to pass a "security awareness test" before s/he can complete the installation process. This method is similar to what some places already require before users can initiate Internet connections on their PC – users must obtain a passing score on a computer security quiz prior to obtaining an Internet Protocol (IP) address. An expanded version of this quiz would allow for the use of an interactive training scenario, as described above. Internet Service Providers could also use this as a means to ensure that their users have knowledge about proper security protections before they first go online.

CONCLUSION

While we pride ourselves on our independence and self-responsibility, especially in the United States, there is only so much we can do to protect ourselves against financial crimes. Personal information, including names, addresses, dates of birth, or telephone numbers, is easily available, whether via the Internet or in a multitude of corporate and financial databases. Social Security Numbers are used on a widespread basis: a SSN may serve as the driver's license number in some states, a student ID number at any number of colleges and universities, or a patient ID number for insurance companies. Given the ubiquitous nature of personal information, I hereby pose the question: "Does IT matter?" Can information technology strategies truly make a difference when it comes to prevention efforts? Even when we are unwilling to give out our Social Security Number over the phone to a utility company, for example, that number is going to be accessible to someone who wants to find it. Similarly, steps we take to protect ourselves may go for naught in the absence of protective measures on the part of the commercial or financial industries. This works to limit how much a person can do to prevent being victimized if a risk factor is beyond his or her control.

In an ideal situation, IT strategies do matter. While these measures may not fully prevent identity theft, even some prevention is better than no prevention at all. But in the end, no matter how strong information technology strategies are, prevention comes down to the human element. Even if technologies are put in place on the server-side, IT becomes worthless the instant an employee answers a question that s/he shouldn't, brings a laptop into work, shares a password, or performs any type of similar activity that jeopardizes the security of personal information. Individuals who don't configure their personal firewall properly or whose computer is powered off during periods when its anti-virus software is trying to update to the latest virus definitions will also not be protected by the technology. Security is only as strong as its weakest link, which highlights the importance of employee and individual training to address weaknesses that IT cannot prevent.

Perhaps the key may be the "illusion of security"; even if IT efforts are not effective in reality, it is more important that they have the appearance of minimizing victimization. Consumer victims have offered a number of recommendations for what they would like to see merchants and financial industries do to assist in prevention, including IT-based measures. It is impossible to say whether their victimization would still have occurred if these measures been in place at the time, but it is also possible that the offender may have been stopped before any identity theft incident could have been initiated. Victims may therefore be less outraged at corporate entities if they felt that some attempt had at least been made to prevent identity theft, either due to good human practices or effective IT measures, instead of doing nothing at all.

What also matters is the need for further research to examine the nature and extent of the problem known as identity theft. Nearly ten years after identity theft was first made a federal crime, we still have minimal data about its victims. The Federal Trade Commission (FTC) has been keeping statistics since 1999, although most of this information only concerns basic victim demographics. Previous major national surveys, including one conducted by Synovate (2003) for the FTC and three longitudinal updates by Javelin Strategy & Research (2005, 2006, 2007) did not address pertinent questions concerning the facilitation of victimization through bad consumer practices or lax guardianship. In the case of the Javelin studies, where some questions were asked about respondent behaviors, only cursory findings have been made publicly available for free. While known survey findings can be used to assist with prevention efforts, the questions being asked of victims or individuals are not designed to make prevention a main goal. Instead of being reactive, surveys should be proactive. They also need to take into account the recommendations made above, especially concerning individual preventative behaviors. Findings must further reflect additional demographic characteristics so that weaknesses in prevention behaviors can be identified within specific populations, thus providing the basis for targeted educational programs.

Identity theft crimes affect millions of Americans each year, presenting a reality that is not easily addressed. We are living in an era where the problem of identity theft is huge and cannot be ignored. Government agencies and research institutions need to step in and ask victims some important questions that will not only find out how this crime has affected them, but discover what behaviors and attitudes may have contributed to their victimization. Prevention and education programs can then be focused on specific population groups and tailored to what they need to learn the most. Finally, the use of information technology strategies should enhance prevention efforts but not minimize the need for human intervention and involvement. Even if identity theft cannot be stopped, various sectors of U.S. society must work together in order to try. This chapter is only a beginning to help us understand this complex problem, but hopefully this discussion has provided some answers towards a solution.

Address correspondence to: Sara Berg, School of Criminal Justice, University at Albany – SUNY, 135 Western Ave., Albany, NY 12222; e-mail: sb872966@albany.edu

Acknowledgments: An earlier version of this chapter appears as: Berg, S. (2006), *Recommendations for a comprehensive identity theft victimization survey framework and information technology prevention strategies*, unpublished Master's thesis, Rochester Institute of Technology, Rochester, NY. The author wishes to thank Dave Clark for his invaluable assistance and review comments.

NOTES

1. A computer virus is probably the best-known type of malware. It is a self-replicating program that, upon execution, will copy itself into any

program it can modify. A worm is also self-replicating, but it can copy itself remotely via connected nodes and does not need a host in which to exist. Trojan is an abbreviation of Trojan horse (from Greek mythology), and it refers to a malicious piece of code that is concealed within an attractive piece of code (Kurzban, 1989).

2. An "exploit" is a type of attack that takes advantage of a computing security vulnerability, such as one found in the operating system or in an application.

3. The term "bot" (short for robot) is a program or set of scripts that appears to be a user connection but is actually automated. It is also possible, however, for an actual IRC user to be their own bot by acting as a file server.

REFERENCES

Center for Problem-Oriented Policing (2006). *Twenty-five techniques of situational crime prevention.* Available at: http://www.popcenter.org/25techniques.htm

Computer Professionals for Social Responsibility (2002, February 14). *CPSR supports Maryland HB281's limits on the use of Social Security Numbers.* Available at: http://ieeeusa.org/policy/policy/2002/02feb14.pdf

Federal Trade Commission (2006, February). "Pretexting: Your personal information revealed." *FTC Facts for Consumers.* Washington, DC: author.

Foreman, J. (2003). "Next Generation: Educational technology versus the lecture." *EDUCAUSE Review*, 38(4):12-22.

Gryphon Foundation (2001, December 27). *Gryphon Foundation Newsletter*, volume 6. Retrieved February 5, 2004 from: http://www.gryphonfoundation.com/winter_2001.htm

Introna, L. and H. Nissenbaum (2000, January). "Defining the Web: The politics of search engines." *Computer* 33(1):54-62.

Javelin Strategy & Research (2005). *2005 Identity Fraud Survey Report: Complimentary version.* Available at: http://www.javelinstrategy.com/

———— (2006). *2006 Identity Fraud Survey Report: Consumer version.* Available at: http://www.javelinstrategy.com/

———— (2007). *2007 Identity Fraud Survey Report – Consumer version: How consumers can protect themselves.* Available at: http://www.javelinstrategy.com/

Kurzban, S. (1989). "Viruses and worms: What can they do?" *ACM SIGSAC Review* 7(1):16-32.

Malik, S. (2002). *Network security principles and practices.* Indianapolis, IN: Cisco Press.

National Center for Victims of Crime (2001). "Identity theft." *GET HELP Series.* Available at: http://www.ncvc.org/

Oppliger, R. (1997). "Internet Security: Firewalls and beyond." *Communications of the ACM* 40(5):92-102.

Saunders, K.M. and B. Zucker (1999). "Counteracting identity fraud in the information age: The Identity Theft and Assumption Deterrence Act. *International Review of Law, Computers, & Technology* 13(2):183-192.

Siemer, J and M.C. Angelides (1995). "Evaluating intelligent tutoring with gaming-simulations." In C. Alexopoulos and K. Kang (Eds.), *Proceedings of the 1995 Winter Simulation Conference*, (pp. 1376-1383). New York, NY: ACM Press.

Sullivan, B. (2004). *Your evil twin*. Hoboken, NJ: John Wiley & Sons.

Synovate (2003). *Federal Trade Commission – Identity Theft Survey Report*. Available at: http://www.ftc.gov/os/2003/09/synovatereport.pdf

U.S. Senate (2000). *Identity theft: How to protect and restore your good name*. Hearing before the Subcommittee on Technology, Terrorism, and Government Information of the Committee on the Judiciary, July 12, 2000. Washington, DC: U.S. Government Printing Office.

Wheatman, V., R. Hunter, L. Behrens, R. De Lotto, and A. Litan (2002, March 8). *Identity theft – The most personal privacy violation*. Available at: http://www.gartner.com

APPLYING SITUATIONAL CRIME PREVENTION TO THE INFORMATION SYSTEMS SECURITY CONTEXT[1]

by

Robert Willison

Department of Informatics
Copenhagen Business School

Abstract: *When addressing computer crime, there is a body of knowledge called Information Systems (IS) security, which aligns itself closely with the goals of Situational Crime Prevention (SCP). IS security practitioners are responsible for defending organisations against a wide range of threats, from hackers to viruses. However, within the organisational context, practitioners must also consider the very real problems posed by employee computer crime. Although a number of IS security researchers have focussed their attention on addressing the "insider" threat, there is currently a lack of insight into the offender/context relationship during the process of committing crimes. Yet, despite the notable similarities, IS security researchers have rarely drawn on criminology – let alone (SCP) – for inspiration or enlightenment. This chapter, therefore, examines how SCP can improve understanding about the offender/context relationship and enhance IS security practices.*

Crime Prevention Studies, volume 23 (2008), pp. 169–192.

INTRODUCTION

When addressing the issue of computer crime, there is a body of knowledge that aligns itself closely with the goals of situational crime prevention (SCP). This body of knowledge – known as Information Systems (IS) security – does not have its origins in criminology, but rather in computer science. Information systems are commonly perceived to consist merely of computers; yet, from an academic perspective, the need to acknowledge the context in which the computers are located and the people who use them have long been recognised (Alter, 2006; Bostrom and Heinenn, 1977a, 1977b; Mumford, 1983, 1995). It is therefore argued that these three elements, and the relationship between them, offer a more holistic and accurate understanding in terms of the design, development and operation of IS.

If this is accepted, then IS security must equally acknowledge and address these factors. Hence, a growing body of work over the last three decades has pointed to the need for addressing security through a "socio-technical" perspective (Backhouse, 1997; Straub and Nance, 1990; Straub and Welke, 1998; Willison, 2006). Password systems are a very simple but highly effective example for illustrating this relationship. The reasons such systems tend to be breached are primarily not technical in nature. Contrary to appropriate security behaviour, many individuals share their passwords with colleagues or write them down and post them on their monitors. A rogue employee may capitalise on this behaviour and access computing resources as a consequence (Adams and Sasse, 1999). Without considering the social element, the problem cannot be properly conceptualised and, as a consequence, cannot be properly addressed.

IS security addresses a considerable range of threats. While the media regularly cover stories of hacker exploits and Internet viruses, these external threats tend to overshadow the very real problems posed by employee computer crime. The related media coverage of the "insider" threat is relatively minor, largely owing to company fears of reputation risk. Even if computer crime is uncovered, organisations are reluctant to bring in law enforcement agencies given the fear of damaged reputations through possible media coverage. Despite this under-reporting, security surveys point to the magnitude of this problem. The 2004 CSI/FBI Computer Crime and Security Survey (CSI/FBI, 2004), based on responses from U.S. companies, revealed that approximately 50% of security breaches occurred within the organisation. These findings are echoed in the 2006 Global

Security Survey by Deloitte (2006), which found that of those organisations that experienced a breach, 49% suffered an internal attack.

More recently, a report by KPMG (2007) examined the profiles of fraudsters. Based on 360 actual incidents investigated by KPMG forensic departments, it was found that 89% involved staff committing fraud against their own employer. From a financial perspective the figures are equally worrying. The 2006 survey by Deloitte reported that 72% of organisations whose security was breached (including external attacks) estimated that the average loss per breach was in the range of $1 million. The Association of Certified Fraud Examiners estimates that organisations in the U.S. lose 6% of their annual revenues through fraud (Ernst and Young, 2004). When compared with the U.S. Gross Domestic Product, this amounts to $600 billion in losses. If realised, such a threat can have a profound effect on the stability of the organisation, and can even lead to its collapse in extreme cases.

The goals of IS security align themselves closely with those of SCP. Newcomers to the IS security field might therefore assume that insights into addressing employee computer crime could be found through the application of criminology, and crime prevention theories more specifically, but this is not the case. A recent review of the IS security literature found that between 1990 and 2004, only ten papers applied criminological theories (Siponen and Willison, 2007). This lack of theory is unfortunately symptomatic of the IS security discipline as a whole. In the aforementioned review, 1,280 papers were analysed, of which over 1,000 were theory-deficient. Although discussed at greater length in the next section, the IS security literature that specifically focuses on the insider threat has made little progress in understanding the offender/context relationship during the commission of employee computer crime.

Given this deficiency and the overwhelming lack of theory in the IS security discipline, this chapter considers the application of SCP to the organisational context. In particular, it is argued that SCP can offer considerable insights and, by so doing, enhance current IS security practices. The first section reviews existing IS security literature that focuses on employee computer crime. This is followed by a discussion of those criminological theories which focus on the causes of criminality, as opposed to SCP, and an assessment of their respective suitability for the IS context. This introduces an examination of SCP, indicating how it can be applied to enhance IS security. There follows the conclusion and suggestions for future research.

LITERATURE REVIEW

A limited number of researchers within the IS security field focus on employee computer crime. The associated literature can be seen to fall into four categories, which include: safeguards, deterring offenders, attributes for offending, and the organisational context. This section reviews this literature and cites existing deficiencies.

Safeguards

A number of writers have discussed the type of controls available for addressing the insider threat (Backhouse and Dhillon, 1995; Dhillon and Moores, 2001; Dhillon et al., 2004; Kesar and Rogerson, 1998). Dhillon and Moores (2001), while noting the need for traditional technical safeguards to regulate access to computing resources, also recognise the need for complementary formal and informal controls. Formal safeguards include written security policies that clarify and dictate the appropriate security behaviour for employees. These are further complemented by informal measures, which cover security education and awareness programmes. Unless a policy is brought to life through educating employees, its effectiveness will be limited. Although articles such as Dhillon and Moores's (2001) have proven important in establishing and recognising the security duties of staff members and how they are established, discussion of the appropriate safeguards for the organisational context remains at an abstract level and provides little guidance for practitioners intent on implementing specific safeguards in equally specific settings.

Deterring Offenders

When discussing controls to overcome employee computer crime, a number of researchers have focussed specifically on deterrent safeguards (Cardinali, 1995; Harrington, 1996; Hoffer and Straub, 1989; Sherizen, 1995; Straub, 1990; Straub and Nance, 1990; Straub and Welke, 1998). In particular, several have applied General Deterrence Theory to the IS security domain. Central to this theory is the role played by sanctions in terms of their perceived certainty and severity by the offender. Hence, the theory postulates that if offenders perceive the certainty and severity of sanctions associated with a crime as high, then this will deter them from engaging in a criminal act. With this is mind, detection and monitoring activities (Hoffer and Straub, 1989; Straub et al., 1992), security and awareness programmes (Straub and Welke, 1998), and codes of ethics (Harrington, 1996) have all been advanced as means by which criminal behaviour can be deterred. Unfortunately, the insights offered by General Deterrence Theory into offender behaviour are limited. Once the offender moves beyond the point of deterrence and engages in criminal behaviour, the theory has little to offer. What is also required is a similar theoretical underpinning for prevention safeguards.

Attributes for Offending

Other writers have considered the insider threat in terms of the attributes required for perpetration (Parker, 1976, 1981, 1998; Wood, 2002). Parker (1998) that argues all "cyber-criminals" should be assessed in terms of the acronym SKRAM, which stands for skills, knowledge, resources, access, and motive. Wood (2002), who specifically focuses on employee computer crime, similarly urges consideration of an offender's skills, knowledge, and motive, but departs from Parker by recommending further consideration of tactics, perpetration processes, and risk avoidance techniques. Unfortunately, both Parker and Wood offer practitioners no guidance as to how any of the aforementioned attributes should be identified and addressed.

The Organisational Context

The organisational context has acted as another source of focus for writers researching the insider threat (Becker, 1981; Sherizen, 1995). An early paper by Becker (1981) asserts the need to focus on the organisational context, as opposed to examining offenders' personalities, in order to overcome employee computer crime. More specifically, Becker argues that dishonest staff perceive the organisational context in a number of different ways, and he provides a classification of seven "criminogenic" environments. Becker further argues that if an organisational context reflects one or more of these classifications, then it will be vulnerable to some form of computer crime. The "land of opportunity," for example, acts as one of the seven environments and represents the organisational context in which dishonest employees are able to exploit vulnerabilities identified during their work. Problematically, Becker does not discuss how offender perceptions are formed, and hence how the individual offender judges whether an environment is criminogenic.

While the aforementioned literature has proven useful in highlighting the problem of employee computer crime, several deficiencies are apparent. The next section discusses the suitability of SCP for application to the organisational context. This is followed by a discussion illustrating how SCP can be applied and, by so doing, addresses the limitations identified in the literature review.

THE SUITABILITY OF SCP FOR THE INFORMATION SYSTEMS CONTEXT

In terms of adoption by the IS security field, criminological theories centered on offender dispositions would appear to offer little. IS security practitioners are not in a position to address the causes of criminality. Even if they were, it is debatable whether the causal factors typically identified by dispositional theories (e.g., socio-economic factors) would account for the criminality of those individuals who perpetrate employee computer crime. By contrast, Clarke (1997:4) notes how:

> Situational prevention comprises opportunity-reducing measures that (1) are directed at highly specific forms of crime, (2) involve the management, design or manipulation of the immediate environment in as systematic and permanent was as possible, (3) make crime more difficult and risky, or less rewarding and excusable as judged by a wide range of offender.

More recently it has also been acknowledged how the environment may "provoke" the offender, and hence a series of techniques have been developed to address such phenomena (Cornish and Clarke, 2003). Given these techniques and the above definition of SCP, the overlap between SCP and IS security is considerable. Indeed, IS security practitioners aim to address potential threats through the application of safeguards in the organisational context. Although discussed in the next section, many of the SCP techniques are already implicitly employed by IS security practitioners. Of fundamental importance – and a common denominator between those individuals who employ SCP techniques and IS security practitioners who address the insider threat – is their ability to manipulate the context in which crimes take place. At a practical level, the advancement of SCP therefore appears well suited to enhancing security efforts that address employee computer crime.

THE APPLICATION OF SCP TO THE INFORMATION SYSTEMS CONTEXT

From an IS security perspective, the 25 SCP techniques advanced by Cornish and Clarke (2003) can be applied to the organisational context for reducing the opportunities for employee computer crime. Table 1 (Willison and Siponen, forthcoming) illustrates an attempt to categorise existing IS security controls using these techniques (for further discussion regarding the prevention of identity theft through SCP techniques, see the chapters by Newman and Berg in this volume). For example, in the group of techniques categorized under "Increasing the Effort" (column 1), the target hardening example (#1) includes "Physical locks for PCs"; hence metal cages and cables are now commonly used for enforcing the physical security of computers. Following are several additional examples of the SCP techniques referenced in Table 1.

Under the SCP category of "Increasing the Risks" (column 2), "Staff chaperoning of visitors" is an example of the "Extending guardianship" (#6) technique. In large companies, it is now standard practice for visitors to be immediately greeted by a receptionist when entering an organisation. Once the visitor has signed-in and been given a visitor's "ID tag" (both of which are examples of # 8: "Reducing anonymity"), the receptionist will then contact the employee who is due to meet the visitor. The employee is then expected to report to the reception desk and escort the visitor to the appropriate office. In this sense, the staff member ensures that the visitor does not enter offices for which he is not allowed access, thereby extending guardianship (#6).

In a bid to enhance security within organisations, companies promote the practice of "Clear desk and computer screen" with the goal of "Removing targets" (#12) and "Reducing the Rewards" (column 3). At the end of the working day, employees are expected to clear their desks and lock away client files, etc. They are also expected to shut down their computers so that sensitive data is not visible on their monitors.

In an attempt to "Discourage imitation" (#20), companies can ensure "Prompt software patching" in order to "Reduce Provocations" (column 4). Whenever new software is released, bugs are inevitably found, which if left un-patched can leave systems vulnerable. Such was the case in 2001, when a bug was reported in an online shopping cart software system called PDG (CSI/FBI, 2002). The bug left customer credit card details exposed on approximately 4,000 websites. Despite the FBI issuing a warning and PDG offering a patch to secure the vulnerability, many companies did not

Table 1: Twenty-Five Techniques of Situational Prevention[a]

Increase the Effort	Increase the Risks	Reduce the Rewards	Reduce Provocations	Remove Excuses
1. Target harden: • **Anti-robbery screens** • *Physical locks for PCs*	6. Extend guardianship: • **"Cocoon" neighbourhood watch** • *Staff chaperoning of visitors*	11. Conceal targets: • **Gender-neutral phone directories** • *Minimise ID of offices*	16. Reduce frustrations and stress: • **Efficient queues and polite service**	21. Set rules: • **Harassment codes** • *Information security policies*
2. Control access to facilities: • **Entry phones** • *Swipe cards for office access*	7. Assist natural surveillance: • **Improved street lighting** • *Open plan offices*	12. Remove targets: • **Removable car radios** • *Clear desk and computer screens*	17. Avoid disputes: • **Reduce crowding in pubs**	22. Post instructions: • **"No Parking"**

Table 1: *(continued)*[a]

Increase the Effort	Increase the Risks	Reduce the Rewards	Reduce Provocations	Remove Excuses
3. Screen exits: • **Export documents** • *Reception desks*	8. Reduce anonymity: • **Taxi driver IDs** • *ID tags for staff*	13. Identify property: • **Cattle branding** • *Property marking*	18. Reduce emotional arousal: • **Controls on violent pornography**	23. Alert conscience: • **Roadside speed display boards**
4. Deflect offenders: • **Street closures** • *Segregation of duties*	9. Utilize place managers: • **Two clerks for convenience stores** • *Management supervision*	14. Disrupt markets: • **Monitor pawn shops**	19. Neutralise peer pressure: • **Disperse troublemakers at school**	24. Assist compliance: • **Easy library checkout** • *Security education for staff*
5. Control tools/weapons: • **Disabling stolen cell phones** • *Deletion of access rights for ex-employees*	10. Strengthen formal surveillance: • **Security guards** • *Intrusion detection systems*	15. Deny benefits: • **Ink merchandise tags** • *Encryption*	20. Discourage imitation: • **Censor details of modus operandi** • *Prompt software patching*	25. Control drugs and alcohol: • **Alcohol-free events**

a. Traditional SCP examples are in bold; italicised examples are from the IS security field.
Source: Willison and Siponen (forthcoming).

take action and the bug was subsequently exploited. Prompt software patching would have fixed the vulnerability, thereby discouraging exploitation and imitation by computer criminals across the Internet.

With respect to the "Remove Excuses" category (column 5), "Information security policies" represent an example from the IS security field for "Setting rules" (#21). Wood (1997) reports the case of an employee who downloaded pornography while at work. When management discovered this activity, the individual was dismissed. However, the individual took his case to a labour board, complaining that he had never been told that downloading pornography was wrong and hence should never have been sacked. The labour board found in his favour and he was subsequently reinstated. An information security policy, which dictates the required behaviour expected of employees, could have prevented this type of situation from occurring.

Given the nature of the organisational setting and the manner in which IS security is enforced, some interesting insights are produced with regard to the application of SCP techniques. More specifically, some of the techniques emphasise the role of third parties for effective security, which further illustrates the redundancy of the idea that IS security is a purely technical concern. The technique entitled "Assist compliance" (#24) illustrates this point. Traditional applications of the technique have focussed on ways to help facilitate expected and appropriate behaviour in a setting. This is in contrast to a situation where the costs in terms of time and convenience may be too high, thus leading to non-compliance. One example cited by Clarke (1997) concerns the manner in which books are checked-out from libraries. Individuals who do not wish to stand in a queue to wait for this service may simply steal the books. Self-service machines assist compliance by enabling individuals to quickly check out the books themselves, hence reducing the number of thefts. In the organisational setting, it is also the case that individuals must comply with rules and procedures – if criminal behaviour occurs, non-compliance is obvious. However, employees are also required to be compliant with security policies in a bid to enforce security. Unfortunately, it is often the case that non-compliance occurs, thus leaving the IS vulnerable. In this sense, the methods for facilitating compliance should be aimed at those required to enforce security and not those attempting to overcome it.

There are two major reasons for non-compliance with an information security policy. First, staff may ignore security procedures, believing that such procedures are unrealistic and hinder their efforts in executing their work responsibilities. So, for example, a password system may require an individual to use four passwords, which must be changed every three months. The security policy may further dictate that all staff must create secure passwords based on a mixture of letters and numbers, and employees must not share them with colleagues or write them down. While staff may be able to create secure passwords, they may find it hard to remember them all. Consequently, passwords may be written down, thereby creating a potential vulnerability. If dishonest employees are aware of such actions, they may exploit the opportunity to their own advantage. As such, a safeguard that is designed to bolster security can in fact weaken it. In this sense, the SCP technique "Assist compliance" could involve the redesign of technical systems and associated procedures. Rather than remembering four passwords, single sign-on systems could be used. These require employees to remember only one password, which greatly reduces the cognitive overheads and makes it much more likely that compliance with related procedures will occur.

Second, it may be that employees are simply not aware of their security responsibilities. An organisation may have a security policy, but unless employees are given the appropriate security education concerning the policy, then it is more than likely that non-compliance will occur. As such, another method for "Assisting compliance" in the organisational context would be "Security education for staff."

This discussion of policies and education also highlights an interesting relationship when considering their classification according to the SCP techniques. Hence security policies can be classified as "Setting rules" and, as noted, security education can "Assist compliance." Given this, it is important to note that a security policy cannot be viewed as a stand-alone measure. Policies will only be effective if they are brought to life by giving staff an appropriate security education.

Selecting Appropriate Safeguards

While the 25 SCP techniques offer IS security practitioners a systematic basis on which to view the range of opportunity reducing options, there still remains the problem of identifying appropriate controls for specific crimes. Admittedly, risk analysis methods have been advocated in the security field for a number of years, but such methods have not been without their critics (Parker, 1998). The problem of safeguard selection is also faced by crime prevention practitioners. In response to this problem, "crime scripts" have been proposed and used to enhance the application of SCP (Cornish, 1994). These scripts afford consideration of a specific crime in its context. In addition, through the use of crime scripts, it is possible to elicit the different stages which constitute the crime-commission sequence. By so doing, offender behaviour is more clearly identified at each stage and this further aids selection of appropriate safeguards. The script approach has been used to address a number of crimes, including check fraud (Lacoste and Tremblay, 2003), body switching (the stealing of motor vehicles for resale purpose; Tremblay et al., 2001), and public transport offences (Smith and Clarke, 2000; also see McNally in this volume for a broader application of the script approach to identity theft).

Willison (2006) has suggested the application of crime scripts to the IS security field as a complement or alternative to risk analysis methods. More specifically, the universal script has been proposed as a tool for their development (Cornish, 1994; Willison, 2006). Table 2 provides an example of the universal script framework (Willison and Siponen, forthcoming). The first column, under the heading "Scene Function," cites the elements of the script, with the corresponding criminal behaviour listed under "Script Action."

The example of criminal behaviour used in Table 2 is taken from the 1998 U.K. Audit Report (Audit Commission, 1998), and refers to a case

Table 2: Universal Script Example

SCENE FUNCTION	SCRIPT ACTION
Preparation	Deliberately gaining access to the organisation
Entry	Already authorised as employee
Pre-Condition	Wait for employees' absence from offices
Instrumental Pre-Condition	Access colleagues' computers
Instrumental Initiation	Access programmes
Instrumental Actualization	False customer account construction
Doing	Authorisation of fictitious invoices
Post Condition	Exit programmes and systems
Exit	Leave offices

Source: Willison and Siponen (forthcoming).

of employee computer fraud. In this instance, several members of a local council department worked with a computerised invoicing system. Individual employees only had access to one part of the invoicing system via their PCs; hence, there was a technical segregation to enhance security. Unfortunately, vulnerabilities were created as a result of employees failing to lock down their PCs prior to leaving the office. This allowed a dishonest employee access to each computer, which facilitated a fraud totalling £15,000. This case further illustrates the need to view IS security as a socio-technical phenomena, for if staff had acted securely and locked down their PCs, then an opportunity would not have existed for the fraudster.

As noted, the IS security literature currently lacks insight into the offender/context relationship during perpetration. The script approach not only allows practitioners the benefit of viewing the criminal act from the offender's perspective, but also allows consideration of the criminal act within the context in which it takes place. Such consideration is further strengthened by the fact that the script approach allows for a systematic review of all the stages in the process of committing crimes, and thus helps to ensure that the criminal behaviour at each stage is identified.

Merging Crime Scripts with the 25 SCP techniques

To facilitate the selection of appropriate safeguards, crime scripts could feasibly be merged with the 25 SCP techniques (Willison and Siponen, forthcoming). By doing so, practitioners would be offered a rigorous and systematic schema for helping to identify not only the criminal behaviour at each stage of the script, but also the appropriate safeguards. Table 3 provides an example of such a merger based on the example of the local council fraud that was just described; the numbers following the examples provided in the SCP columns represent the specific techniques outlined in Table 1.

As noted, the need for viewing IS security from a socio-technical standpoint allows for a consideration of the relationships among safeguards, honest employees, and potential offenders. Furthermore, scripts and the SCP techniques can potentially aid conceptualisation of the inter-relationships among the three. In the case of the local council fraud, scripts help to identify the criminal behaviour and the SCP techniques offer a range of safeguard options. However, they also allow practitioners to consider scenarios where non-compliant behaviour by honest employees leads to security vulnerabilities that may be exploited by potential offenders. Hence,

Table 3: The Merger of a Script with the Twenty-Five SCP Techniques

Scene function	ScriptK action	Increase the Effort	Increase the Risks	Reduce the Rewards	Reduce Provocations	Remove Excuses
Preparation	Deliberately gaining access to organisation	Prospective employment screening (4)				
Entry	Already authorised as employee					
Pre-condition	Wait for employees' absence from offices	Physical segregation of duties (4) Staggered breaks (4)	Signing in/out of offices (8)			
Instrumental Pre-condition	Access colleagues' computers	System time outs (2) Biometric fingerprint authentication (2)				Information security polices (21) Security education (24)

Table 3: *(continued)*

Scene function	ScriptK action	Increase the Effort	Increase the Risks	Reduce the Rewards	Reduce Provocations	Remove Excuses
Instrumental Initiation	Access programmes	Password use for access to specific programmes (2)				
Instrumental Actualization	False customer account construction		Two person sign-off on new accounts (9)			
Doing	Authorisation of fictitious invoices		Audit of computer logs (8) Budget monitoring (8)			
Post-condition	Exit programmes					
Exit	Exit system		User event viewer (8)			
Doing Later	Spend the transferred money					

Source: Willison and Siponen, (forthcoming).

consideration can be given to the prerequisites, which are required for staff to correctly execute their security responsibilities.

In Table 3, the script "Pre-condition" (row 3) involves the script action of "Wait for Employees' Absence." Under the heading "Increase the Risks" (column 4) is the safeguard of "Signing in/out of offices." Underpinning the enactment of this control is an understanding that staff will conform to this safeguard. To help assist compliance, there should be not only an information security policy, but also the appropriate education so that staff understand their security responsibilities and act upon them accordingly. This is also the case with the "Instrumental Pre-Condition" (Table 3, row 4), where PCs need to be locked down in order to "Increase the Effort" (Table 1, #1). Once again, this requires not only a security policy, but also education and awareness efforts. However, if staff are non-compliant, the merged script/SCP techniques allow practitioners to consider redundant or alternative safeguard options. In Table 3, if staff fail to lock down their PC's, then the redundant control of system time-outs could be implemented where the computer automatically locks down after a certain period of time. Alternative safeguards could include, for example, biometric fingerprint authentication. Rather than having to input a user name and password for access, the honest employee simply has their thumb or finger scanned to allow for access to computing resources.

Offender Attributes

One additional benefit of the script approach concerns the identification of offender attributes. The existing IS security literature notes the need for considering attributes (Parker, 1998; Wood, 2002), but fails to explain how they should be studied and addressed. Because scripts allow for an examination of a specific crime in its context, this further allows for an examination of the attributes used for perpetration. This is largely due to the fact that the criminal context plays a large role in defining and dictating the required attributes.

Rather than using the terms "attributes," Cornish and Clarke refer to "choice-structuring properties," defined as "those single or multiple features of particular criminal activities which make them differentially available and attractive to certain individuals at certain times" (Cornish and Clarke, 1989:108). Hence, the perceived rewards and costs will play a large role in determining whether the specific crime is "attractive" to certain individuals in specific contexts.

What makes the insider threat so potentially devastating is the employees' enhanced ability to determine what is "attractive" and what isn't. This point can be elaborated by referring to the concept of bounded rationality, which forms one of the six propositions advanced in the rational choice perspective (Clarke and Cornish, 2000). As noted by Clarke and Cornish (ibid: 25), the rational choice perspective assumes that:

> . . . an individual's behaviour is characterised by "limited" or "bounded" rationality. That is to say that criminal decision making is inevitably less than perfect because it reflects imperfect conditions under which it naturally occurs. Because offending involves risk and uncertainty, offenders are rarely in possession of all the necessary facts about costs and benefits (the risks, efforts, and rewards of crime). Although they try to act as effectively as they can, choices may have to be made quickly and revised hastily.

Because dishonest staff are employed in the context in which they commit crime, they are much more likely to be in "possession of all the necessary facts about costs and benefits." Insiders may well have a very good knowledge of existing safeguards and vulnerabilities. As a result of being employed in a potentially criminal context, insiders also have the added luxury of time to assess their environment and form their choices.

Importantly, apart from articulating the offender behaviour at each stage of the script, consideration can also be given to the choice-structuring properties that underpin the criminal behaviour. Just as the script approach allows practitioners to consider the prerequisites for compliant security behaviour by honest staff (e.g., a security policy and security education and awareness programmes), so too does it allow for consideration of the prerequisites for criminal behaviour. For example, in terms of the local council fraud, not only did the offender require knowledge of the security vulnerabilities (i.e., the failure of his colleagues to lock-down their PCs), he also required computer and accounting skills to process the fraud. Without these skills, the crime would not have appeared "attractive" to the offender. Of some significance here are the implications for prevention practices, since cases of employee computer crime demonstrate how skills are acquired in the workplace setting for the execution of legitimate employment responsibilities, and then used by rogue staff for illegal gain. However, because dishonest employees glean these skills in the organisational domain, consideration could perhaps be given to denying access to such skills. Just as a division of duties aims to deflect offenders, division of skills could possibly be used in a similar manner.

CONCLUSION AND FUTURE RESEARCH

When addressing computer crime, IS security aligns itself closely with the goals of SCP. IS security practitioners are responsible for defending organisations from a plethora of threats including viruses and hackers. However, within the organisational context, this group of practitioners must also address the problems posed by employee computer crime. While a number of IS security researchers have focussed their attention on the "insider" threat, there is currently a lack of insight into the offender/context relationship during the commission process. Yet despite the commonalities, IS security has rarely drawn on criminology – let alone SCP – for inspiration or enlightenment. This chapter has therefore examined how SCP can help to provide an understanding of the offender/context relationship, and subsequently enhance IS security practices.

The 25 SCP techniques can be seen to offer IS security practitioners a systematic basis from which to view the range of opportunity-reducing options. However, practitioners are still faced with the problem of identifying appropriate controls for addressing specific crimes. In response to this problem, the use of crime scripts has been proposed because such scripts afford considerable insight into the offender/context relationship. They allow practitioners to view the criminal act from the offender's perspective, and within the context in which it takes place. Practitioners are further aided by the fact that the script approach enables a systematic review of all the stages in the commission process. This helps to ensure that all of the behaviour at each stage is identified. To assist in the overview of scripts and SCP techniques, the two could even be merged to provide a rigorous and systematic schema (see Table 3).

As discussed, a socio-technical approach to IS security allows for a consideration of the relationships among safeguards, honest employees, and potential offenders. Scripts and the SCP techniques also aid in the conceptualisation of the interrelationships among the three. For example, in the example above involving the local council fraud, scripts help to identify the criminal behaviour and the SCP techniques offer a range of safeguard options. However, they also allow practitioners to assess where non-compliant behaviour by honest employees leads to security vulnerabilities, which could possibly be exploited by potential offenders. As a consequence, consideration can be given to the prerequisites (such as security policies, and security education and awareness programmes), which are necessary if staff are to fulfil their security responsibilities.

One final benefit of the script approach is its ability to locate specific crimes in specific contexts, thereby helping to identify the choice-structuring properties. This is largely owing to the fact that the criminal context plays a sizeable role in defining and dictating such properties. Hence, at each stage of a script, an assessment can be made of the associated choice structuring properties that underpin the behaviour.

From an academic perspective, the 25 SCP techniques open up potentially new avenues for research. As can be seen in Table 1, there are a limited number of IS security controls classified under the heading "Reduce Provocations" (column 4) and "Remove Excuses" (column 5). It is debatable whether all the techniques could be applied to the IS domain, given that their development has addressed a number of different crimes in an equally diverse number of contexts. The "Disrupt markets" (#14) and "Reduce emotional arousal" (#18) techniques are cases in point. Yet even these techniques should not be rejected outright; rather consideration should at least be given to how they have been previously applied in other contexts in order to determine their potential for the IS context. Other techniques, however, obviously display more promise.

At a broader level, the techniques that fall under the heading "Reduce Provocations" allow us to consider the extent to which the organisational context provokes potential offenders. Of some significance is the recognition that if the organisational context does provoke offending, then some potential exists for addressing causal factors. Potential inroads into this area could possibly be made by drawing upon theories that focus on the issue of "fairness" within organisations. This concept has been addressed by a group of theories, which collectively fall under the umbrella term "organisational justice" (Greenberg, 1990a; Skarlicki and Folger, 1997; Skarlicki et al., 1999). In particular, there are three main theories that examine different organisational phenomena influencing employees' perceptions of fairness: "distributive," "procedural" and "interactional" justice. Distributive justice focuses on the perceived fairness by employees of the rewards (outcomes) they receive for their contributions (inputs) in comparison with other colleagues (Adams, 1965; Greenberg, 1990a). Procedural justice focuses on the fairness perceptions associated with the policies and procedures used to determine the aforementioned outcomes (Folger and Greenberg, 1985; Lind and Tyler, 1988; Tyler and Bies, 1990). Finally, interactional justice addresses fairness perceptions of an employee in terms of, for example, respectfulness, consistency, and sensitivity from those in positions of authority.

Importantly, studies researching all the three forms of organisational justice have confirmed their roles in influencing perceptions of fairness in the corporate environment (Skarlicki and Folger, 1997; Skarlicki et al., 1999). Of particular importance to the current discussion is additional research that has studied the relationship between employee perceptions of fairness and organisational deviance. Several studies have focussed on organisational justice and "revenge" (Bies and Tripp, 1996), "retaliation" (Skarlicki and Folger, 1997; Skarlicki et al., 1999), and "theft" (Greenberg, 1990b, 1993).

Table 1 further illustrates the lack of IS security safeguards, which can be classified under the heading "Remove Excuses." The process by which potential offenders rationalise their behaviour in an attempt to absolve themselves of guilt and shame has received relatively little attention from the IS security field (Harrington, 1996; Sherizen, 1995), but it has been argued that a more systematic research agenda may open up a potentially fruitful area for the implementation of safeguards (Willison, 2006). Indeed, the organisational context appears especially suited, since:

> . . . techniques designed to induce guilt and social embarrassment may prove particularly useful for crimes involving relatively uncommitted offenders, such as those involved in minor acts of juvenile delinquency, and white-collar crimes, where the offender can be assumed to have a considerable stake in conformity. (Wortley, 1996:129)

Initial IS security research efforts could possibly involve an attempt to identify the range of rationalisation methods used by employee computer criminals. A taxonomy for guiding more focussed prevention efforts could then be developed.

This chapter has demonstrated that SCP offers considerable value to the IS security field, but the benefits do not only flow one way. When SCP is applied to new areas, the insights gained can have implications for other fields. A case in point concerns the technique "Assist compliance" (Table 1, #24). Traditional applications have focussed upon efforts to assist the potential offender to conform to the appropriate and expected pattern of behaviour. In this text, it has been noted how "Assisting compliance" also has relevance for staff for who are central to enforcing security. If the procedures are considered impractical, or staff are simply not aware of their security responsibilities, then non-compliance may occur and vulnerabilities can be created as a result. Obviously, third parties are also responsible for other forms of security in a whole range of areas and the potential insights garnered from one field can be useful for enlightening the application of SCP in others.

Address correspondence to: Robert Willison, Department of Informatics, Copenhagen Business School, Howitzvej 60, DK - 2000 Frederiksberg, Denmark; e-mail: rw.inf@cbs.dk

NOTES

1. *Editors' note* – It may surprise some readers to realize that the term "identity theft" does not appear anywhere in this chapter. This is due, in part, to the author's focus on the safeguarding of personal information, rather than its misuse. The acquisition of personal information is nevertheless vital to the commission of identity theft, and the author's discussion of situational crime prevention in this context enhances our understanding of this process.

REFERENCES

Adams, J. (1965). "Inequity in social exchange." In: L. Berkowitz (Ed.), *Advances in Experimental Social Psychology*. New York, NY: Academic Press.

Adams, A. and M. Sasse (1999). "Users are not the enemy." *Communications of the ACM* 42:41-46.

Alter, S. (2006). *The work system method, connecting people, processes, and IT for business results*. Larkspur, CA: Work System Press.

Audit Commission (1998). *Ghost in the machine: An analysis of IT fraud and abuse*. London, UK: Audit Commission Publications.

Backhouse, J. (1997). "Information at risk." *Information Strategy* January:33-35.

Backhouse, J. and G. Dhillon (1995). "Managing computer crime: A research outlook." *Computers and Security* 14:645-651.

Becker, J. (1981). "Who are the computer criminals?" *ACM SIGCAS Computers and Society* 12:18-20.

Bies, R. and J. Moag (1986). "Interactional justice: Communication criteria of fairness." In R. Lewicki, B. Sheppard and M. Bazerman (Eds.), *Research on Negotiation in Organizations*. Greenwich, CT: JAI Press.

Bies, R. and T. Trip (1996). " 'Getting even' and the need for revenge." In R. Kramer and T. Tyler (Eds.), *Trust in Organizations: Frontiers of Theory and Research*. London, UK: Sage Publications.

Bostrom, R. and J. Heinen (1997). "MIS problems and failures: A socio-technical perspective, Part I: The causes." *MIS Quarterly* 1:17-32.

———— (1997). "MIS problems and failures: A socio-technical perspective, Part II: The application of socio-technical theory." *MIS Quarterly* 1:11-28.

CSI/FBI (2002). *Computer crime and security survey*. San Francisco, CA: Computer Security Institute.

—— (2004). *Computer crime and security survey*. San Francisco, CA: CSI.

Cardinali, R. (1995). "Reinforcing our moral vision: Examining the relationship between unethical behaviour and computer crime." *Work Study* 44:11-17.

Clarke, R. (Ed.), (1997). *Situational crime prevention: Successful case studies* (2nd ed.). Monsey, NY: Criminal Justice Press.

Clarke, R. and D. Cornish. (2000). "Rational choice." In R. Paternoster and R. Bachman (Eds.), *Explaining Criminals and Crime: Essays in Contemporary Criminological Theory*. Los Angeles, CA: Roxbury Publishing Company.

Cornish, D. (1994). "The procedural analysis of offending and its relevance for situational prevention." In R. Clarke (Ed.), *Crime Prevention Studies*, vol. 3. Monsey, NY: Criminal Justice Press.

Cornish, D. and R. Clarke (1989). "Crime specialisation, crime displacement and rational choice theory." In H. Wegener, F. Losel, and J. Haisch (Eds.), *Criminal Behavior and the Justice System: Psychological Perspectives*. New York, NY: Springer-Verlag.

Cornish, D. and R. Clarke (2003). "Opportunities, precipitators and criminal decisions: A reply to Wortley's critique of situational crime prevention." In M. Smith and D. Cornish (Eds.), *Theory for Practice in Situational Crime Prevention*. (Crime Prevention Studies, vol. 16.) Monsey, NY: Criminal Justice Press.

Deloitte (2006). *Global Security Survey*. Available at: http://www.deloitte.com/dtt/cda/doc/content/us_fsi_150606globalsecuritysurvey(1).pdf

Dhillon, G. and S. Moores (2001). "Computer crimes: Theorizing about the enemy within." *Computers and Security* 20:715-723.

Dhillow, G., L. Silva and J. Backhouse (2004). "Computer crime at CEFORMA: A case study." *International Journal of Information Management* 24: 551-561.

Ernst and Young (2004). *Global information security survey*. Available at: http://www.ey.com/global/download.nsf/UK%20/Survey_-_Global_Information_Security_04/$file/EY_GISS_%202004_EYG.pdf

Folger, R. and J. Greenberg (1985). "Procedural justice: An interpretive analysis of personnel systems." In K. Rowland and G. Ferris (Eds.), *Research in Personnel and Human Resource Management*. Greenwich, CT: JAI Press.

Greenberg, J. (1990a). "Organizational justice: Yesterday, today, and tomorrow." *Journal of Management* 16:399-432.

—— (1990b). "Employee Theft as a Reaction to Underpayment Inequity: The Hidden Costs of Pay Cuts." *Journal of Applied Psychology* 75:561-568.

—— (1993). "Stealing in the name of justice: Informational and interpersonal moderators of theft reactions to underpayment inequity." *Organizational Behavior and Human Decision Processes* 54:84-103.

Harrington, S. (1996). "The effects of ethics and personal denial of responsibility on computer abuse judgements and intentions." *MIS Quarterly* 20:257-277.

Hoffer, J. and D. Straub (1989). "The 9 to 5 underground: Are you policing computer crimes?" *Sloan Management Review* 30:35-43.

KPMG (2007). *Profile of a fraudster survey*. Available at: http://www.kpmg.co.uk/pubs/ProfileofaFraudsterSurvey(we b).pdf

Kesar, S. and S. Rogerson (1998). "Developing ethical practices to minimize computer misuse." *Social Science Computer Review* 16:240-251.

Lacoste, J. and P. Tremblay (2003). "Crime and innovation: A script analysis of patterns in check forgery." In M. Smith, and D. Cornish (Eds.), *Theory for Practice in Situational Crime Prevention*. (Crime Prevention Studies, vol. 16.) Monsey, NY: Criminal Justice Press.

Lind, E. and T. Tyler (1988). *The social psychology of procedural justice*. New York: Plenum.

Mumford, E. (1983). *Designing human systems for new technology: The ETHICS method*. Manchester, UK: Manchester Business School Press.

————— (1995). *Effective systems design and requirements analysis – The ETHICS approach*. Basingstoke, UK: Macmillan Press.

Parker, D. (1976). *Crime by computer*. New York: Charles Scribner's Sons.

————— (1981). *Computer security management*. Reston, VA: Reston Publishing Company, Inc.

————— (1998). *Fighting computer crime: A new framework for protecting information*. New York: Wiley Computer Publishing.

Sherizen, S. (1995). "Can computer crime be deterred?" *Security Journal* 6:177-181.

Siponen, M. and R. Willison (2007). "A critical assessment of IS security research between 1990-2004." In the proceedings of the 15th *European Conference of Information Systems*, St. Gallen, Switzerland, June 7-9, 2007.

Skarlicki, D. and R. Folger (1997). "Retaliation in the workplace: The roles of distributive, procedural, and interactional justice." *Journal of Applied Psychology* 82:434-443.

Skarlicki, D., R. Folger and P. Tesluk (1999). "Personality as a moderator in the relationship between fairness and retaliation." *Academy of Management Journal*, 42(1):100-108.

Smith, M. and R. Clarke (2000). "Crime and public transport." In M. Tonry (Ed.), *Crime and Justice: An Annual Review of Research*, vol. 27. Chicago, IL: University of Chicago.

Straub, D. (1990). "Effective IS security: An empirical study." *Information Systems Research* 1:255-276.

Straub, D., P. Carlson and E. Jones (1992). "Deterring highly motivated computer abusers: A field experiment in computer security." In G. Gable and W. Caelli (Eds.), *IT Security: The Needs for International Cooperation*. Amsterdam, Netherlands: Elsevier Science Publishers.

Straub, D., and W. Nance (1990). "Discovering and disciplining computer abuse in organisations: A field study." *MIS Quarterly* 14:45-60.

Straub, D. and R. Welke (1998). "Coping with systems risks: Security planning models for management decision making." *MIS Quarterly* 22:441-469.

Tremblay, P., B. Talon and D. Hurley (2001). "Bodyswitching and related adaptations in the resale of stolen vehicles." *British Journal of Criminology* 41:561-579.

Tyler, T. and R. Bies (1990) "Beyond formal procedures: The interpersonal context of procedural justice." In J. Carroll (Ed.), *Applied Social Psychology in Business Settings*. Hillsdale, NJ: Erlbaum.

Willison, R. (2006). "Understanding the perpetration of employee computer crime in the organisational context." *Information and Organization* 16:304-324.

Willison, R. and M. Siponen (forthcoming). "Overcoming the insider: Reducing employee computer crime through situational crime prevention." *Communications of the ACM*.

Wood, B. (2002). *An insider threat model for adversary simulation*. Menlo Park, CA: SRI International.

Wood, C. (1997). "Policies alone do not constitute a sufficient awareness effort." *Computer Fraud and Security* December:14-19.

Wortley, R. (1996). "Guilt, shame and situational crime prevention." In R. Homel (Ed.), *The Politics and Practice of Situational Crime Prevention*. (Crime Prevention Studies, vol. 5.) Monsey, NY: Criminal Justice Press.